Lifestyle Lost

By David A. Umling

Constructing our Pendleton County Retirement House (2011)

This book is dedicated to all people who seek truth and meaning from a self-reliant lifestyle.

Written and produced by David A. Umling – December 22, 2011

Printed by Kindle Direct Publishing – Seattle, WA

Library of Congress Control Number - 2020909042

With great appreciation for editorial assistance and support from Frank O'Hara, Paul DePalatis, Phil Hager, Michael Morgan, Jon Boone, Larry Thomas, and my loving wife.

First Printing – 2012 (Xlibris)

Second Printing – 2020 (Kindle Direct Publishing)

About this book and its author...

Drawing upon his diverse life experiences, David Umling carries you on an engaging odyssey as he describes the two lifestyles he has lived—his childhood experiences growing up on a small family hardscrabble farm in the Appalachian Mountains and his adult professional life as a city planner. He recounts, in loving detail, the influential experiences and traditional folkways from his upbringing and how they shaped his understanding of the life he lived and the outside world into which he transitioned.

David's childhood stories teach us of the virtues and practical benefits of the self-reliant, homespun Appalachian culture and lifestyle that nurtured him, but that he never fully realized and appreciated until later in life. The story follows his journey into adulthood and the struggles he faced adapting to life in modern society and reconciling it with the core values he internalized as a child. Through his achievements, disappointments, and personal reflections, David compares and contrasts the two distinct lifestyles he has lived. His insights reveal how the lessons he learned persuaded him to pursue a simpler and more traditional lifestyle in the mountains of Pendleton County, West Virginia. In the process, he gives us an enlightening perspective on our society, how we live within it and how it ultimately defines us.

David lives with his wife of 21 years, Barbara, and their 20-year-old son, Michael, in New Creek, West Virginia. From that home base, they are working to build their future retirement home in Pendleton County. David is the city planner for Cumberland, Maryland, a job he has held since 2007. David earned a Bachelor's Degree in Sociology and a Certificate in Applied Social Research from the University of Hartford, Connecticut in 1984 and a Master's Degree in City Planning from the University of California at Berkeley in 1986. In 2004, he received the Distinguished Leadership in planning award from the Alabama Chapter of the American Planning Association. Having lived the first eighteen years of his life on a dairy farm, David has been an outspoken advocate for rural communities and their special needs within the planning field.

Table of Contents:

I. Foreword

Since my wife and I bought our core retirement property in Pendleton County, WV in the fall of 2006, I have read nearly 100 books on Appalachian history, culture, and traditional folkways. Many of the books I have read focus on the customs, lifestyles, and folkways of the Potomac Highlands region of West Virginia and, where the literature exists, Pendleton County. I have an intense interest in the traditional ways of my adopted home here because they are so familiar to me and the memories I still have of the place where I grew up. You see, I wasn't born or raised in the West Virginia highlands I have come to love and cherish. I was born in another part of the Appalachian Mountains that was equally sheltered from the modern ways of living and technology that most urban Americans embrace and accept as normal and proper.

I was raised on a family-operated, hardscrabble dairy farm that was only 100 miles removed from the modern urban society (by road), but was almost completely sheltered from it. We often referred to that society as the "outside world" because it was so different to us. Our farm was tucked away in a river valley that divides two states. We were completely surrounded by the foothills of the Appalachian Mountains and isolated by a lifestyle that kept us close to the land and the small villages and towns that were neatly nestled within them. We lived at the edge of poverty by outside standards, but never felt deprived nor did we fail to satisfy our basic needs. Our lives were not much different from those around us, so if we lived in plight, it was a plight that we all shared and never recognized or internalized as such. Now that I have read so much about West Virginia and its cultural heritage, I understand that my childhood home and its setting were no different from, and could easily have been mistaken for, a missing pocket of West Virginia. At that time, I never would have described our little region as being part of Appalachia, but I now realize and accept that it was, both culturally and economically.

Having never spent any meaningful time in West Virginia before purchasing our retirement property, my understanding of the state was based solely on the prevailing narrow media representation of the state and region. To me, West Virginia was a coal mining state with perpetually impoverished people living in tiny, dirty coal company shacks and economically enslaved by their debts to the company store. The popular media never explained the breadth and depth of the state's diverse environment and its cultural heritage.

West Virginia's heritage extends far beyond coal wars, slurry dam failures, and company towns. Her beautiful and seemingly boundless mountain landscape has nurtured a wide variety of self-reliant economic pursuits and lifestyles that testify to the rugged independence and determined pride of her people. While it is true that most of her people live very modest lifestyles, they are not all trapped in the state by poverty. Many of them *choose* and *prefer* to live a simpler life that keeps them close to nature and their family traditions. They are justifiably proud of their innate ability to carve a satisfying, honest life out of the rugged land. Their wealth is not derived from or measured by the money they earn or possess, but from the satisfaction they gain by living close to nature in a peaceful and serene setting.

Many West Virginians do not possess a high level of formal education, but that doesn't make them stupid or ignorant. What they may lack in formal education is more than compensated by their knowledge of how to live a self-reliant lifestyle and survive off the land. Such people have lifetime skills that would make an M.I.T.-educated physicist in the woods look like a bumbling idiot. If the modern American economy were to collapse tomorrow, most intellectual urban-dwellers would quickly learn how valuable and important those basic skills truly are.

The rugged mountain landscape of West Virginia means more to her people than something pretty to behold and appreciate. The diverse forests; deep and dramatic hollows; boundless mountaintop ridges; and the swift, clear, cold mountain springs and streams are an intimate and meaningful part of their traditional lifestyles and homespun culture. The landscape provides bountiful sustenance and a strong sense of place and home that distinguishes daily life from the commercialized placelessness of the outside modern world. Hunting, fishing, sanging (harvesting ginseng), and collecting the various wild and prolific fruits of the land—from ramps to nuts—are ingrained into and inseparable from the traditional folkways and lifestyles. The mountains also provide a reassuring sense of orientation—of always knowing where you are by reading the surrounding landscape. The state's natural, mountain landscape is an endowment to West Virginia's future generations that must be passed along with the culture, for it would have no meaning, context, or inherent value without it.

Having grown up in the same mountains, I have an innate understanding of these emotional and cultural ties to the landscape. To me, West Virginia is not just another state; it's a state of mind and a lifestyle that I recognize, understand, and appreciate. That's why I ultimately decided to complete my life here. I may not be *from* West Virginia, but I *chose* to live here, and I will be as stubborn to uproot or displace as any multi-generational native of the state would be. West Virginia is a natural fit for me and my core values, so it is easy for me to feel the same sense of pride in this place as any true native.

So, why am I telling you all this? As I learn to have a greater understanding and appreciation for the lifestyle and folkways that defined my upbringing, I realize how rare they have become and how threatened they are with extinction. Modern urban life, with all its wealth, glamour, technology, and convenience, has—in my opinion—eroded and displaced the traditional ways and culture. It has created what I call a "society of dependency" or "interdependency," which some may prefer as a more positive label for this alternative lifestyle. From my perspective, this society is distinctly different from the "society of self-reliance" that defines traditional rural West Virginia (Appalachian) lifestyles and that made me who I am and now choose to be.

Before I start using the terms "society of self-reliance" and "self-reliant lifestyle" too many times, let me be clear about what I'm really saying. I'm sure some clever person would argue that a society of self-reliance is a contradiction in terms, because anyone who was completely self-reliant would be living alone in the wilderness and could hardly be part of a larger society. Moreover, anyone who chooses to become part of a larger community must compromise some element of his/her own independence in order to be a good and considerate neighbor. However, that is a reasonable argument only if you take the term "self-reliant" to the extreme.

Lifestyle Lost

I assert that a person can live a self-reliant *lifestyle* without necessarily living independently in the wilderness in the same way that we can all live in a free society without literally having the complete freedom to do *anything* we wish *any time* we please. There are many people who have lived the extreme form of a self-reliant lifestyle, like the pioneer families who first settled the Appalachian Mountain wilderness nearly 300 years ago. However, I recognize the fact that a self-reliant lifestyle is more than just one person living alone in the wilderness. It's a pattern of traditional rural living that is tied close to the land and is based on core values of dedicated hard work and pride in self-achievement—much as the Native Americans lived for thousands of years before European colonization. These are the cornerstone values I learned growing up on a farm, and they represent the basic lifestyle we lived and *chose* to live.

I should also make it clear that I don't mean to suggest or assert that my childhood experiences are the standard or ideal measure of a self-reliant lifestyle. We did not sustain our own lives without support from the larger "outside" society and economy. We had to buy fuel for our vehicles and farm equipment that we could never produce on our own. We bought grain for our cows because we couldn't grow all of the feed they needed to produce quality milk. We sold our milk to a commercial dairy and earned money from it, even as we did not receive an hourly wage or salary. We may not have been the best farmers, but we did do our best.

Perhaps there are no totally self-sustaining people left in today's society. Even the Amish use telephones (even though most still do not have one in their homes) and allow people to drive them where they need to go for work. Still, they exemplify the spirit of independent living that drives or supports a self-reliant lifestyle, and that is what I internalized from my childhood experiences. I just didn't accept that for many years. I have now come to realize that I possess that spirit, and it both drives and is nurtured by the core values I gained from my childhood.

To me, the two different lifestyles that I am discussing are not either-or propositions, but should be conceived as varying degrees on a broad and continuous spectrum of self-sufficiency or independence. There are always varying *degrees* of self-sufficiency. I think the distinction is like the modern political spectrum, where one can be a Republican or a Democrat even though there remains a much wider range of political thought and perspectives that extends well beyond those two parties and their specific platforms. Many people like me who are in the middle (political independents) have political perspectives that cross party lines or define the issues quite differently. We just lack an organized, official party platform, or a specific party affiliation. The societies of self-reliance and dependency that I am discussing can be more appropriately understood as fundamental approaches to living that lead to different lifestyles.

In my view, people who deliberately seek to provide for their own needs to the greatest extent possible and enjoy living independently as a core value can be said to be living or pursuing a self-reliant lifestyle. They are part of the society of self-reliance that I am discussing. On the other hand, people who are motivated to accumulate wealth and seek social standing within the context of a money-based economy can be said to be living in or pursuing a lifestyle of dependency or social interdependency. When compared to my earlier example of the political spectrum, the distinction I intend to draw between the two societies is more akin to conservative and liberal ideologies than to Republican or Democratic parties. In that sense, the values associated with each political ideology *inclines* that person to prefer one party (or lifestyle) or the other—but does not necessarily dictate it.

For example, consider the Amish and the "back-to-the-land movement." Both can be said to represent strongly self-reliant lifestyles as I am defining them. On one side of the coin, the Amish exemplify a very conservative society based firmly in religious principles and conducted through the application of very traditional technology and folkways. On the other side of the coin, the back-to-the-land movement emerged directly out of the radically liberal hippie and "free-speech" movements of the late 1960s. In drawing my analogy, I am not suggesting that either lifestyle should be tied to one political ideology or the other. I am merely using political concepts as an example to explain the distinction I am trying to draw between the two different lifestyles and the societies they represent.

It occurs to me that our modern urban society and economy have become so complicated, grand in scale, and reliant (dependent) on wealth and technology that average citizens don't know how to sustain themselves without it. Regrettably, I have lived most of my adult life within it, and I still don't have a clue of how to fix my computer or car if they break down, strategically invest what little wealth I have, or treat simple ailments. The technology I have grown accustomed to using and depend upon to earn a living doesn't necessarily empower me to be more self-reliant. In many ways, it only makes me more dependent on others to satisfy my basic needs.

My college education taught me, as it does everyone else, to be a specialist within the larger society. I learned to be a city and regional planner, and that is what I do. Since 2007, I have served as the city planner for Cumberland, Maryland. Over the past 25 years, my planning career has been the source of my income, which allows me to purchase the services of other specialists to address the basic needs that I don't know how or wish to satisfy on my own. I suppose some would say, "That's the beauty of the system." To me, it represents a serious weakness that—should our modern, urban economy collapse—would devastate most of its benefactors and potentially lead to lawlessness, starvation, and extensive helplessness. It is the wealth of the market economy that makes the system work and masks its fundamental weaknesses. It allows our society to grow and develop to the very boundaries of its ability to sustain itself.

But, does that technologically advanced and enchanting urban economy really create a fundamentally better and more sustainable society than the society of self-reliance that it actively supplants and destroys? As I internalize the influences it has had on me and the people around me, it has made us lazy (and inherently overweight and unhealthy), vain, materialistic, casually wasteful, isolated from the natural environment, and dependent on others to fulfill our basic needs. Is that what we truly call progress, sophistication, and enlightenment?

When I left the farm and entered the outside modern urban society, I was not prepared for the lifestyle changes I would have to make. I have told my wife many times that the life we live does not seem "real" to me. I just wasn't able to clearly convey what I meant to a person who was raised in a city. Now I understand it from the perspective of the basic differences between the two societies I have experienced, the society of self-reliance that I came from and the society of dependency into which I had moved.

My feelings weren't a simple reaction to the culture shock that such a drastic transition promotes. It was the feeling of helplessness and the dependency on money (which is not something that my upbringing taught me was inherently dependable) that I couldn't easily adjust to or accept. I had to wear a suit and tie and learn to speak formally. That was something I could learn to do, but it felt like wearing a costume. It was something that I put on to play the role and comply with my employer's expectations, but that didn't fit or reflect the person I really was.

As a child, I was raised to look up to and respect the few people in our area who wore stylish suits and spoke formally. "Those are the people who have improved themselves by getting an education and working hard. They are the decent people that society has rewarded for their efforts and that we should strive to be." That's what we were always taught and, not having any meaningful interaction with that world or lifestyle, I accepted as self-evident.

However, I have dealt directly with many wealthy people who wear suits, speak formally, and have advanced educations. In my planning experience, I have learned that many of them are far from virtuous in their basic values and have enriched themselves by taking advantage of others who did not know or appreciate the true value of their land or resources. Their specialized knowledge empowers them to cleverly profit from others who lack knowledge about land development or its potential value—probably because they have their own different skills and specializations. This realization was devastating to the core values that I internalized as a child and made the real world feel far less real to me.

I would like to feel the promise of Martin Luther King, Jr.'s speech, when he dreamt of a day when people would be judged not by the color of their skin (or, as I would expand upon it, the wealth they have earned), but by the "content of their character." However, in my experience living within what I call the society of dependency, that would only expose one of its fatal flaws. Wealth often appears to be a greater reward for skill and cunning than it is for virtue and high moral character. This inconvenient truth often makes me wonder what money is truly worth. Perhaps that is why most people seem so inclined to spend it so liberally on material goods that only serve to validate and inflate their personal vanities.

I guess the statements I have just expressed make me sound very critical of modern society, but I am what my experiences and core values have taught me to be. Those who know me best realize that I tend to be very direct and forthright. I hope that you won't judge me or what I have to say until you have gained a better and more intimate understanding of both lifestyles. I speak from that experience. I only seek to whet your appetite to consider something different than you may have ever experienced.

I am not writing this book as an intellectual research paper on the technical differences between the two societies I have characterized. I simply want to tell the story of what my experiences in these two societies have taught me and why I feel the society of self-reliance is inherently *valuable* and should be cherished and *made relevant* in our modern, technologically sophisticated society. I don't seek to instill a sense of pity for the erosion that has occurred as the more traditional lifestyles have faded. That is *not* the way that anyone who lives a self-reliant lifestyle would wish to be perceived. I would prefer to instill an awareness of the inherent value that this alternative lifestyle offers, and I hope that it will entice more people to actively choose to pursue it. Only in that way will it continue with integrity and meaning, rather than as a museum exhibit or a fond but quaint memory.

The simpler ways of living do not have value simply because they are rare or different. They have value because they remind us more intimately of our place in the natural order and reward us with a greater appreciation for the environment that sustains us and defines who and what we really are. I feel that, in doing so, those who live a self-reliant lifestyle are inherently less pretentious. For the self-reliant West Virginians who read this story, I offer it as respect from one who gets it. I'm sure *you* will understand what I mean.

Yes, I do have a bias, but I certainly didn't begin my adult life with it. Quite the opposite, I eagerly entered the society of dependency and even tried for years to adjust my thinking to embrace it. In my early years, I often avoided discussing details of my background in professional circles to avoid the embarrassment of disbelief and the stigma of being perceived as a backwoods hick. I have only recently (over the past twelve years) learned to accept and become comfortable with the values and experiences I gained from my childhood. The impressions of our modern society and economy that I offer in this story were forged from lifelong experiences and polished smooth through personal contemplation and reflection.

As the reader, it is your right to decide if you will agree with what I say or not. While what I have to say is as honest as I can be, that does not make it the final word on the subject. I don't expect to convince anyone to change his/her views, if my experiences don't warrant that. I simply ask for the right to express my views on the subject as my contribution to a broader understanding of these two different lifestyles. I don't doubt that there may be more alternative lifestyles that deserve discussion. Unfortunately, these are the only two I've lived, so I don't feel qualified to express my thoughts on any others. If you have those experiences I lack, please feel free to write your own story. Perhaps I will choose to read it.

Now, I'm sure that some of you are wondering why I haven't revealed precisely where I was raised. I have a good reason for that. As you will recall, I made the assertion that my childhood home is a cultural and economic twin to West Virginia and could even be thought of as a separate part of Appalachia. If I told you where that was up front, you might be initially inclined to reject that assertion. I have faced that reaction for many years, dating back to when I was attending college. Many people my age wouldn't believe the stories I told about my childhood life because they could not accept that someone could grow up that way in the 1960s and 1970s— especially in that area. However, everything I have to tell you about how we lived is true and largely verifiable by others who lived there at that time. As a result, I would like to withhold that bit of information until I have told you more about the setting and lifestyle that framed my childhood. Then you can decide for yourself without the bias of knowing the location. Once I have explained those two aspects of my childhood, I will reveal where it is. If I can request your indulgence, let me introduce you to my own little slice of Appalachia. By the way, I'm not the only person I know who would freely agree with that characterization.

Replica of Colonial Fort at Number 4 (2011)

The "Clickety-Click Bridge (2011)

The Setting

I was raised on a 120-acre dairy farm that stretched along a river that divided two states. The farm was located immediately north of and across a small tributary stream from the village center of my community. This village was not an incorporated place, so I can't tell you exactly what its population was, but I would guess that it wasn't much more than 150. When you add in all of the neighboring areas that were identified with the village, the population increased to about 750. During my childhood years, outsiders (flatlanders from the coast and out-of-staters, as we called them) were beginning to move into our area. That was the beginning of the end for our traditional farming community.

Farming was still one of the economic pillars of my area while I was growing up. Most of the farms were dairy operations, although there were still a number of apple orchards, horse farms, and poultry farms—none of which were large-scale operations. Other major economic pursuits included a number of heavy industries that produced precision tools and a forest products industry that included timber companies, lumber mills, and paper mills (mainly producing paper bags, particleboard, and cardboard boxes).

Roughly 50 years before I was born, logging was a much larger industry and the spring log drives that ran down our river would stretch for 50 miles. Loggers would follow the drive down the river using long wooden boats called "bateaux" and rafts carrying horses to break up logjams. A small number of textile mills remained, but they were in decline. The primary products those mills produced were wool clothing and shoes. Small-scale gravel mining operations also existed in our area. The largest local gravel operation was located in our neighboring village. It was owned and operated by the largest family in town, which also owned a farm on the outskirts of the community. They had a total of thirteen surviving children, so they had plenty of workers to operate an expanding business.

Most people are not aware of this, but the primary historic base of employment in most rural areas has been manufacturing, not agriculture or forestry. While agriculture and forestry uses are land-intensive and represent the predominant features on the landscape and a significant source of income within rural communities, they don't provide a majority of rural jobs.

This mistaken belief was confirmed by a 2001 survey on suburban and urban perceptions of rural America conducted for the W.K. Kellogg Foundation by Greenburg-Quinlan-Rosner Research. The resulting report entitled, <u>Perceptions of Rural America</u>, provides a thought-provoking and enlightening assessment of non-rural perceptions and misperceptions of rural living of which my farming experiences represent but one of many different aspects.

The Kellogg survey results showed that respondents generally perceived rural America as being based almost completely on an agricultural economy even though direct farm employment only constitutes, on average, about seven percent of all rural employment. When related support jobs are added, the employment total increases to slightly less than twelve percent.[i] Although we were not one of them, a number of small family farmers in my area supplemented their farm incomes by working part-time jobs in the area's manufacturing plants or by operating their own cottage businesses.

My childhood experiences tend to reflect common public perceptions of rural and Appalachian lifestyles, but they really weren't as common as most people may presume—especially in today's society. The modern agricultural economy is increasingly dominated by large-scale specialized and highly mechanized commercial or industrial farms. In contrast, my farm upbringing was more characteristic of an increasingly rare lifestyle that tends to be confined to economically isolated or remote communities in which small, functionally-diverse family or subsistence farm operations predominate. This more traditional farming pattern is far better suited to the difficult and challenging Appalachian region terrain and soils than it is to other agricultural regions of the country.

The two largest communities in our immediate area had total populations of about 13,000 and 10,000. The larger community was an incorporated city, while the other was a large town. What stores and businesses they offered were our primary sources of outside supplies, equipment, and parts for our farm equipment. Large national chain stores and restaurants were only just beginning to take root in our area when I was growing up and only in these two larger communities. (I can still remember when the first McDonalds restaurant opened in our area.)

Most of our immediate relatives lived in the larger community, the downtown of which was six miles north of our farm. Most of our routine business needs were served by this city, but like most people who lived in the river valley, we conducted business on both sides of the river.

The smaller community was located to our west and across the river in the opposing state. Our milk was sold to and collected by Idlenot Dairy, which was headquartered in that town. While its downtown was closer to our farm as the crow flies, it was an eleven-mile drive away because it could only be reached by crossing one of the few bridges that spanned the river. The bridge to this town was an old, two-lane truss bridge officially known as the Cheshire Toll Bridge. The tires of our car would click as we drove over the joints in the bridge's original wooden decking, so we always jokingly referred to it as the "clickety-click bridge" (see photo on page 10). That name won't have much meaning to current generations because the bridge decking has been upgraded a number of times since then.

One of the bridge's travel lanes was occupied by railroad tracks, and if a train was coming, you had to wait for it to cross before you could drive safely to the other side. Some people would enjoy the thrill of racing across the bridge to beat the train or dodge the tollbooth (to evade the toll) on our side of the bridge after dark. We would learn of some of those people and their brave and daring exploits a few days later by reading the obituary section of the local paper. A few of them made it necessary for the tollbooth to be regularly maintained or reconstructed. Not surprisingly, the owners of the bridge didn't like to maintain or rebuild the tollbooth that frequently, so they eventually built a tall concrete barrier in front of it. That improvement reduced the maintenance work to occasionally patching and repainting the barrier. Sometimes, you can't motivate people to change their behavior no matter what you do.

Our farm was seven miles north of the larger main village in the center of our town. This village was the center of government and services for the town and was located at our end of the clickety-click bridge. Its population was around 1,500 when I was growing up. Many of our childhood friends from school lived in and around the town's main village.

Lifestyle Lost

Our town was on the very fringe of British control during the French and Indian War, and the main village grew around a frontier fort that played a significant role in repelling superior French forces during that war. A relocated period reproduction of that fort is located very close to the clickety-click bridge and serves as the town's primary tourist attraction.

The town even had its own "Mary Draper Ingles" story of Indian raid, capture, and enslavement associated with the war and the fort. In 1754, a band of Indians raided the community and captured Susannah Johnson and members of her family, who lived just outside the fort. They and the other captives were forced to march over a hundred miles up the river into French territory, where they were enslaved and divided into various Indian families. Some of the hostages were placed in a French prison. Mrs. Johnson gave birth to a baby two days into the march. One of the other captives was killed and allegedly cannibalized by the Indians along the way. After four years of captivity, all of the Johnsons gained their freedom and returned safely to the community. Extensive permanent settlement of the area did not begin to take hold until after that war ended.

Our own village was really more of a hamlet than a full-scale village. A two-lane state highway named the River Road, but depicted on official maps as state route 12-A, connected us to the village and the larger world beyond. It was the main highway for north/south travel on our side of the river until it was bypassed by a straighter (and higher speed) two-lane state highway in the 1960s. As a very young child, my father would drive me to the road construction project to watch all of the heavy equipment. I would refer to the large and noisy earthmovers as "rum-rums" because of the strained sound their engines made struggling to carve out and level the roadway. It was the single biggest development project that occurred in my town throughout my childhood.

The center of our little hamlet consisted of a small, two-room, stone schoolhouse, a Methodist Church, and a Grange Hall (which was slowly deteriorating from a lack of regular use and routine maintenance). At one time in the past, the village had a post office and a store, but the building that housed them was long empty by the time I was born. The building remains today, but it is in a sad state of disrepair. Scattered modest 19th and early 20th century homes filled in the gaps within our tiny village. Some of them are now gone and the yards have overgrown in mature trees. It's hard for one to believe that there was ever a building on those lots, and you would have to look hard to find the original cellar holes.

The village also had a public burial ground named Hope Hill Cemetery. We lived very close to the cemetery, and the town would give our family the key to the main entrance gate every spring so we could open it in the mornings and lock it at night. I would often tell people that we were the "keepers of the keep." We had to walk up the hill into the cemetery each evening before locking the gate to make sure that no one was accidentally locked inside. Somehow, despite our best efforts, people would still get locked in at night— but only one time. It's one thing to visit a cemetery, but quite another to realize that you can't get out after dark.

One winter as a child, a friend and I once decided to go sliding down the icy cemetery access road on a runner sled. It was quite steep in places and the lower half of the road was a straight shot, so it looked like fun. We learned on the first trip down why that was not a good idea. We had built up such speed coming down the icy drive that we were afraid we wouldn't be able to stop at the bottom to avoid sliding out into the main road. We veered to the right to avoid the intersection and ran into some loose barbed wire fencing that had been left at the corner of our field from the previous spring. Life on the farm was often difficult and dangerous, so lessons like that (and getting locked in the cemetery) only had to be learned once.

The village school was the focus of our community and the source of its pride. Jessie Farwell, a wealthy benefactor from the village who had long since moved away to Detroit, financed its construction. It was built in 1889 to replace four one-room schoolhouses that were scattered around the community. The school is an imposing structure with a huge stone archway at the entrance and a tall belfry. In its early years, the school housed all nine grades. The graduating students in the late 1800s and early 1900s wrote their names and graduation years in the red mortar between the massive stones that formed the entranceway arch. As small children just beginning our formal schooling, we would marvel at the size of the students who had left their marks. However, by the time I attended the school to begin first grade, its enrollment was being reduced to just the first three grades. I have many memories of my brief years at that school some of which I will discuss later in this story.

The broader region along the river was what I would call intensely hilly. When I worked as a surveyor's assistant one summer during my college years, I determined that the land in my state was either on a mountain or in a swamp. The biggest mountain in our immediate area was located in the opposing state and rose to a height of about 3,150 feet, but it was the only real mountain that actually bordered the river. It was ten miles north of our house, and it was the commanding centerpiece of the views from every window and door on the front side of the house. Several mountains within 25 miles of our farm rose from heights of 2,500 feet up to 3,300 feet but we couldn't see them directly from our property. We were located in what I would call the foothills between two major mountain ranges—one in each state. Since our farm was in the river bottom that divided the two ranges, our elevation was only about 350 feet above sea level, and views of the higher mountains beyond were blocked by the low hills and bluffs that channeled the river.

In my readings of Appalachian books, I came across an excellent description of the physical setting of the area where I was raised. The author is Scott Hastings, Jr., who was the founding curator of a regional farm museum that was created to preserve the culture, traditions, and folkways of my area. In one of his books, published in 1990, he gave the following description of my little Highlands area. I inserted my own wording in the parentheses that follow to replace any detailed identifying information. His description in his own words, I believe, supports my statements about the incredible physical similarities between the area where I was raised and my adopted area of West Virginia. To be precise, our farm was located a few miles south of the area he describes, but it shared the same characteristics, even throughout my childhood. You may find his description a bit more formal than mine.

"Before my work could begin, however, it was necessary to establish the geographical boundaries for the region I needed to study. The...Highlands will not be found on any map but the one in this book. The territory is some thirty or forty miles wide by sixty miles long, the western

border lying along the crest of the...Mountains (west of the river). *Eastward, the land descends in a confusion of rough, broken hills, and mountains. These promontories are intersected and pushed back by a labyrinthine maze of deep, narrow valleys, through which rush swift streams and rivers...With* (the main) *river, the concept of a culturally cohesive region spills over into the valley towns* (east of the river). *Close ties have always existed between* (the river towns in the two states).

"The population of the...Highlands is concentrated in the towns and large farms along the river. In the hills rising steeply from the river intervales, farms and villages are smaller. A few farms are sited on the hilltops; the valley slopes being given over to rough pasture and woodlots. This backcountry exists on a scale nicely fitted to humans; a fact often commented on by the observant outsider. The hills confine the sky so that it is small. Fields are small, too, and often stony and sharply tilted. Fields encompass every bit of arable land. For that reason, they fit no standard field pattern but are irregularly shaped. Along the valley bottoms it is the same—here the fields assume their shapes from being crowded against the wooded ridges. It is no uncommon thing to find that a hill has pinched off a field, pushing the narrow dirt road beside it onto a slim overhang above the stream below.

"Prolonged isolation on remote mountain farms and villages helped preserve the patterns of life originally brought from the British Isles, then subjected to one hundred and fifty years of adaptation to conditions of life (along) *the Atlantic* (Coast. This area, along with both states, were) *the first American frontier after the initial settlement of the colonies. It is this fact, together with a harsh climate and a loose settlement pattern of scattered farms and villages...that has been responsible for the persistence of an independent frontier cast of mind lasting well into the twentieth century. Even now* (the 1970s), *among the older generation, this mindset has not entirely disappeared."*[ii]

That is how Scott Hastings described it, and that's how it was when I grew up on the farm. Do these descriptions make it easier for you to guess where it is? Perhaps now you can understand why I feel that my childhood home would fit equally well in the Potomac Highlands of West Virginia. Well, the truth of the matter is that what I have described to you is the Upper Connecticut River Valley of New Hampshire and Vermont. Our farm was located in the village of North Charlestown, which is part of the town of Charlestown. At one time in the distant past, I learned that an effort was made to make North Charlestown a separate town, but it failed in the state's legislature by one or two votes.

The two largest communities that I described were the city of Claremont, NH and the town of Springfield, VT, respectively. The 3,150-foot mountain that borders the Connecticut River is Vermont's Mount Ascutney. That mountain and the Connecticut River Valley divide the Green Mountains in Vermont from the White Mountains in New Hampshire.

The village school in North Charlestown is the Farwell School which, not surprisingly, is listed on the National Register of Historic Places. The pioneer fort in Charlestown is the Fort at Number 4. Isn't that a classy name? When it was first settled, Charlestown was known only as "Plantation Number 4." It didn't receive its current name until after the French and Indian war. The fort and the village of Charlestown were key strategic outposts during that war—just like Forts Seybert and Upper Tract in Pendleton County, WV. In fact, Charlestown was the northernmost British settlement in the Connecticut River Valley at that time. During the summer tourist seasons, the reconstructed fort is operated as a living history museum with costumed interpreters.

Scott Hastings' description of the Upper Valley region was from his book, <u>The Last Yankees</u>, in which he names that area the Yankee Highlands. The farm museum he started is the Billings Farm and Museum in Woodstock, VT. At first, I didn't really care for the name he gave to my region. My wife and I lived in Georgia and Alabama for thirteen years, and we understand the negative connotations associated with the term, Yankee. Yet, after I moved to the Keyser area in 2008, my good friend, Frank O'Hara, began referring to me as an old New England Yankee. Later, he loaned his copies of two of Scott Hastings' books to me, and I began to understand his reasons for calling me that. He wasn't using it as a derogatory or sarcastic term (as it is frequently understood in the deep south). He was talking with respect and reverence for my traditional values, pragmatic rural northern New England outlook, and crusty, sarcastic sense of humor. Once I learned that, I felt more comfortable with his characterization. I guess I can't deny that is a fair assessment of my character. With the love I feel for my newly adopted state, I hope that someday, I can be accepted as an honorary native West Virginia Yankee. To me, that would be the greatest honor and distinction that has ever been bestowed upon me.

Now you can truly understand where I was raised. I hope that the descriptive similarities will make it easier for people in traditional Appalachia to associate with the story I am about to tell of my childhood experiences in the Yankee Highlands. As you read about them, please bear in mind that my childhood years *began* at least twenty years after the Great Depression ended. Nevertheless, some of the aspects of our lifestyle may sound eerily reminiscent of that era. If I had lived in that area during the Great Depression, my childhood experiences would have sounded as though I was talking about the latter half of the nineteenth century. If you don't believe me, just read another of Scott Hastings' books, <u>Goodbye Highland Yankee</u>. Those were his childhood experiences from that era. Thank you for lending me those books, Frank. You are the first person I have met from outside my area (including my own wife) to realize and accept that I was telling the truth about it after all.

My Childhood Farmhouse (2011)

III. How We Lived – *Growing Up in the Appalachian Society of Self-Reliance*

Before I begin discussing my childhood experiences, I need to briefly explain the unusual circumstances of my family background. Although I was raised in a traditional rural family setting with a mother, father, and four sisters, our relationships were not as traditional as they might appear to the casual outside observer. The two oldest children (me and the eldest of the four girls) were adopted into the family. The three younger girls (the youngest of which was precisely 13 ½ years younger than me) were our parents' biological children. Our family had considerable difficulties dealing with the adopted girl who appeared to be developmentally disabled and socially challenged. She was prone to fits of unpredictable behavior and was very late to mature.

During our early years, our parents argued frequently over how to deal with the adopted girl's developmental problems. Occasionally, these arguments would focus on the different ways that our adopted parents were treating the two adoptees. The four eldest children (the two adoptees and the two eldest biological daughters) would overhear these arguments between our parents. The third biological daughter was born after these arguments ceased, and her experiences within the family were quite different from the rest of us.

Over time, the disagreements caused a rift between the adopted and biological children. The eldest biological daughter often resented our presence in her family because of the division it caused between her parents. After one especially loud and bitter argument, she vented her frustrations by confronting me and her adopted sister and telling us that she didn't consider us legitimate members of her family because we weren't born into it, and if it wasn't for us, her parents wouldn't argue so much. There was no way to deny her statement, and it made me feel very conscientious and guilty about my adoption into the family. This rift between the older adopted and younger biological children was never openly discussed or resolved and only grew deeper over time. The eldest biological daughter eventually became jealous of the responsibilities placed on me as the family's only son. She felt that it somehow interfered or competed with her relationship with her mother. Our family's inability to resolve and overcome the bitter feelings only led to other arguments and disagreements that never made any sense, but were the only way to vent the pent-up frustrations.

By the time we became adults, it was clear that we would never be able to get beyond the bitter division that had grown between us. After my adoptive father died in 1984 and the farm was sold in 1986, we gradually drifted apart and went our separate ways. Both my adopted sister and I had left New Hampshire by 1990 and had only limited interactions with the family thereafter. My adoptive sister never received any treatment or support for her developmental problems and led a broken life that frequently left her in trouble with the law, addicted to alcohol and drugs, and pregnant with an out-of-wedlock child that she was not capable of raising. Another member of my adoptive family eventually adopted that child.

The end of my relationship with the eldest of the family's biological daughters came in 1995, when I learned that she had blamed me for causing her mother's breast cancer. They were still in New Hampshire at that time, and I had been living in Georgia since 1991. As I said, none of the issues we argued about ever made any more sense than that. They were merely excuses to vent bitter feelings and resentments because we couldn't find a way to discuss the real issues that divided us. By then, I was fed up with the endless bickering. As my wife (Barbara) correctly observed, my relationship with my adoptive family was like trying to mix oil and water.

As I grew older, I began to experience health problems that could not be precisely diagnosed. Like all adoptees, I had no biological family medical history to give my doctors any direction to identify the root causes. After our only son, Michael, was born in 1991, I began to be concerned that he might inherit my medical problems and would need to know more about his biological medical history than I could provide. Concern about these issues and my own long-standing, natural curiosity about the fundamental differences between my adoptive family and me eventually made me consider seeking my biological roots.

Lifestyle Lost

So, in 1998, I searched for and found my biological family. In doing so, I discovered that my biological family was completely intact and that I was a middle child in that family. This situation is extremely rare in adoption cases. Most adoptions arise from out-of-wedlock births, broken families, or child abuse cases and usually involve either the oldest child or all children in the family. As it turned out, there were flaws in my adoption process, about which my adoptive parents apparently had some knowledge that they hid from me. Before the adoption was finalized, my biological father had tried to intervene and regain custody of me. I was born and adopted in 1962, and during that era, procedural errors like this were not made public. The New Hampshire Department of Health and Human Services responded to the issue by denying my father's objections, waiving certain procedural requirements, and expediting my adoption case.

As you might expect, my decision to search and the information I learned from it did not sit well with my adoptive family and especially with my adoptive mother. After a few tense conversations about the situation, she gave me an ultimatum. I had to decide which family I would associate with: hers or my biological family. After all the divisiveness, lies, and secrecy that clouded my relationship with my adoptive family and the receptivity and acceptance that I received from my biological family, I chose the latter. By the end of 1998, I was officially readopted by my biological parents, and my original family name was restored.

I can say with firm conviction that I did not casually turn away from my adoptive family. Now that I have been in close contact with my biological family for the past twelve years, I can also report that I am not close to all of my biological brothers and sisters. They also have their own lingering childhood issues to deal with, and they don't all get along well. In a real twist of irony, one of my biological sisters could not accept me any better than my adoptive family sister. My biological sister refused to accept me as her brother because I didn't grow up with *her* family. In this case, the adoption factor had the opposite effect that it did in my adoptive family. Since I can't change the fact that I was born into a family I didn't grow up with and was subsequently raised by a family I wasn't born into, which family am I truly entitled to be a part of? Who is best qualified to decide that for me, the Department of Health and Human Services, or other people who don't know me or my situation? Who you would want to make that decision for you?

Lifestyle Lost

For several years after my re-adoption, I stayed in contact with four of my adoptive relatives who understood and supported the reasons for my decision. However, it became clear over time that my contact with them was placing them in the middle of a bitter and inherently unresolvable debate, so I eventually decided to let go of them as well. After all, they still had to live within that family. Since then, I have had no further contact with my adoptive family.

My 1998 re-adoption helps protect my adoptive family's identity. I have chosen not to identify them by name in this book because the situation has been difficult and painful enough for *all* involved. In other words, none of us wants to go there again. From my perspective, it is important to understand that we are all a product of *both* our environment and genetics. For most people, those fundamental influences reside in one family. However, I am an adoptee, and those influences will be forever divided into two separate families. My medical history and physical traits can be understood only through my biological family. On the other hand, my environment and childhood values were determined exclusively by my experiences with my adoptive family. To be forced to choose between both of them is like being required to decide which arm you would prefer to have amputated. Further details of my adoption experiences are discussed in my 2014 book, <u>Reflections on My Lives</u>.

Despite the personal difficulties we faced in my adoptive family, we were all profoundly influenced by the rural, traditional lifestyle we lived. It is those shared experiences that form the basis for the story I wish to tell in this book. Like all families, we had our good and bad times, and we all learned the values of hard work and self-reliance. I still carry those memories and values with me today, regardless of my last name or which family I associate with. They continue to be and will always be an important part of me. In fact, I have come to understand how those values also make me different from some of my biological brothers and sisters. I now have a better and more complete understanding of who I am and how I came to be. That knowledge has been a source of strength and confidence in my personal choices over the twelve years that have passed since my re-adoption. It also contributed to my decision to live a more self-reliant lifestyle and retire in West Virginia. In that respect, it has influenced my decision to tell you this story, and it would be incomplete if I didn't explain it.

I cannot simply ignore or abandon the memories and experiences I had with my adoptive family any more than a divorcee can simply forget the influential experiences and memories from a long marriage. In the final analysis, we all face difficult choices in life. We can only choose to let them impede us in our growth process or learn from them and adapt accordingly. When you seek to live a self-reliant lifestyle, you have to learn to confront the difficult decisions, make a rational, deliberate choice, and live with the consequences, regardless of what they may be. For it is *not* the consequences of your decisions that ultimately define your character; it is the determination and personal integrity you show by facing them *despite* the consequences.

I've often heard people say, "You can't choose your family." In my case, I was faced with that difficult and unenviable choice. Please don't treat that lightly until you have had to face it for yourself. I won't claim I made the choice that others might feel was right, but I made the right one for me at that time. Regardless of the quality of the individual relationships I now have or will ever have with either my adoptive or biological families, I managed to gain from them a better understanding of who I am and how my experiences in life have shaped me. That, too, is part of the learning process, and I continue to benefit from it. That is also the benefit one can hope to achieve from a self-reliant lifestyle.

Now that I have explained this aspect of my childhood background, I would like to tell you more about how we lived. After all, that is the most important and relevant aspect of my childhood experiences to this story.

****

As a child, I was told that our farm began its life in 1791 as a rural highway tavern. It was allegedly built and operated by the brother of one of the state's early governors. I simply can't confirm that information. The oldest main section of the wood-framed, two-story house, which was oriented parallel to the highway, was designed in authentic colonial style. A brick extension was added sometime in the early 1800s.

Lifestyle Lost

The house's early history as a tavern is somewhat supported by the fact that there were four large granite hitching posts (each of which was about four feet tall above the ground and separated about six feet apart) running in a straight line in the front yard between the house and the highway. Drilled holes located roughly waste high on each post marked the former locations where forged iron eye hooks were bolted (all but one of which had long since rotted away or were eventually removed) and through which a roughly eighteen-foot length of heavy iron chain was stretched to use when tying up horses between the house and the road. The area was just being settled at that time, and it seems reasonable to me that four granite hitching posts were more than one family would need to temporarily tie up horses outside the house. Along the highway just beyond our farm (adjacent to Ox Brook) there also was an old spring-fed stone water trough for horses that operated throughout my childhood. We would occasionally drink fresh water from it as we walked past on our way to the village.

The old stone water trough was removed many years ago, and I don't know exactly what happened to it. Sometime later, I was told that a stone trough is now stored in the shed behind the Farwell School. I don't ever recall seeing one in that building when I lived in the area. It is entirely possible that they are one and the same. It wouldn't surprise me because that shed held a number of relics from the past. When I was growing up, I recall opening the carriage doors of that shed to reveal a horse-drawn, steam-powered fire wagon from sometime around the turn of the twentieth century that was stored inside. I don't know if it's still there.

What I do know is that, when my adoptive parents purchased our farm in 1960, the previous owners had operated it as a family dairy farm for several generations. In fact, their operation had once included chickens and horses, as well as cows. The farm complex included a long chicken house and a horse barn, both of which collapsed in later years because we didn't actively use those buildings and couldn't afford to maintain them.

Our farming operation was limited exclusively to milk production, and aside from a running series of family dogs, cats, and two geese (named Eek and Meek), we kept no other farm animals. About 30-32 of our cows were actively producing milk at any given point in time. All but one of them were Holsteins. We always tried to keep at least one Jersey in our milking herd to raise the butterfat levels of our milk. We also had anywhere between five and ten calves and heifers (cows that had not reached adult milking stage). The youngest calves would be kept with their mothers for their first few days or in a special room in the barn. After they were nearly six months old, we would place them in an outdoor pen in front of the barn. The males would eventually be sold off as breeding stock or for meat (veal). Sometimes, we would keep the meat. The females would eventually be added to the milking herd after they had given birth and were ready to produce milk. We did not keep bulls to breed our cows; we hired an artificial inseminator to take care of that and ensure our cows were bred by a stud with a good lineage of producing milking cows.

Breeding our cows was often a problem in the early years because we couldn't be sure we could place a call to the artificial inseminator in time. Our telephone service was a party line that was shared by six homes in the village. My father always complained that Mrs. Snelling would tie up the phone line all day talking to her friends so no one else could place a call. And if she wasn't talking, she was secretly listening to someone else's conversation so she'd have something to gossip about afterward. I think most of those old rural party telephone lines had a Mrs. Snelling. After all, someone had to be the life of the party.

Only the first floor of our farmhouse was heated. The only air conditioning system we had was a gentle mountain breeze that occasionally wafted through the house when the windows were open. Heating the house was the primary concern because freezing temperatures would typically begin in September and last well into May. We did have warm and pleasant summers, but they were often very short. As we were fond of saying, they usually occurred on a Wednesday.

The house's central heating system was an oil-fired radiant hot water furnace that was located in the cellar. It circulated hot water through a series of baseboard copper pipes that ran along the exterior walls of the first floor. Since the house was poorly insulated (as you might expect from a true colonial-era home) and the winters were so long and cold, the system had a very difficult time heating the house. The system's hot water would cool rapidly as it circulated around the drafty foundation, leaving many of the rooms (including my bedroom) cooler than most people would comfortably tolerate today. We tried to keep the house warmer in the winters by raking fall leaves into large, black lawn and leaf garbage bags and stacking them around the house foundation. This made a difference, but nothing could completely stop the determined New Hampshire winter cold from finding its way into the house. I typically wore flannel long johns (Johnson Woolies), flannel shirts, sweatshirts, or sweaters in the house throughout the long cold winters just to be comfortable.

The second floor was completely unheated throughout my childhood, but many of these rooms were actively used even during the winter months. As the oldest and only (surviving) male child, I was first to have my own bedroom. It was a very small room that was converted from an old mud room adjacent to a former side entrance that was sealed off many years before we lived there. The girls all eventually moved into larger upstairs bedrooms. Over the years, all of us had the experience of spending winter nights in those unheated second floor bedrooms.

I remember one Christmas in 1984 or 1985 when I returned home from graduate school in coastal California. I had to sleep in one of those upstairs bedrooms because our grandmother was spending the holiday with us, and she had taken my old bedroom. At that time, I was acclimated to temperatures in the San Francisco Bay area that routinely climbed into the low 60s during the day and came home to sleep in an unheated bedroom when the night-time temperatures dropped to 26 degrees below zero. I climbed into the bed fully clothed and undressed beneath four layers of blankets and a quilt. I kept the quilt pulled over my head while I was sleeping, but when I would roll over, the cold of the pillow against my cheeks would wake me up every time. After I awoke in the morning, I got dressed under the covers before braving the freezing temperatures in the room. When I did get up, I noticed that the morning sun was filtered by a thick layer of frost that had built up on the *insides* of the windows. Many times, during the winter we would find a thin layer of fine snow on the window sills that had blown through small gaps between the window sashes.

Sleeping in these winter conditions was made possible by outdated technology (in combination with thick skin and flannel sleepwear). Since the central furnace could not adequately heat our house on its own, we also had a cast iron Home Comfort wood-fired cookstove in the kitchen. It was built in 1857 by the Wrought Iron Range Company of St. Louis, MO. The stove had a central oven with a marginally responsive temperature gauge, a main firebox, a large cooking surface and two small, side-by-side bread ovens at the top. It was designed for a hot water tank mounted to the side, but it was long gone when we inherited it. The oven doors and trim pieces were finished in a creamy yellow color with decorative bundles of wheat painted on them. It was a beautiful and functional antique heirloom that had served as the centerpiece of the large open kitchen for generations. This stove and the kitchen it heated were the main focus of our winter existence. We spent lots of time working in the kitchen or sitting around the kitchen table in front of the stove. It was the only room in the house that always remained warm (especially when the power went out), and we would keep that stove burning, as best we could, throughout the long winter nights.

To heat the upstairs beds, we would place several large soapstone bricks (roughly one-foot square in size and about two inches thick) into the woodstove oven and heat them throughout the day. In the evenings, roughly an hour before going to bed, we would carefully slide the hot blocks out of the oven and wrap them in bathroom towels secured by safety pins. Then, we'd carry the warm, tightly wrapped stones upstairs and slide them under the cover and blankets to warm it well before climbing into bed. The stones would keep the bed warm more than long enough to help you get to sleep, no matter how cold the air in the room would get.

The house sat on a stone foundation that extended below ground to the base of the cellar. The cellar had a bare earth floor throughout and several side rooms that were used for cold storage. It was a perfect winter storage location because it was always cold and dank—even during the summer months. We used the side storage rooms to store the firewood that we burned in the kitchen stove during the winter. We also stored all of the vegetables we canned or salvaged from our garden on wooden shelves and in a potato crib that lined the walls of the cellar. An old well that once served the house flowed into a brick-lined water tank in the cellar. While the tank held water all the time we lived there, we never used it, and it remained covered by heavy wooden planks.

Lifestyle Lost

The farmhouse stood before a large farm complex, consisting of seven other structures. The main structure was the milking barn with an attached silo, which we used to store corn silage through most of my childhood. The barn had a wide central concrete aisle that ran the length of the building, dividing it into identical holding and feeding areas on both sides for our milking cows. On either side of this aisle were opposing concrete feed trenches backed by rows of stanchions capable of holding, if I recall correctly, up to sixteen cows on each side. That's why our milking herd was never greater than 32 cows. Each cow had its own assigned stanchion, and they knew exactly where to go when we brought them into the barn for the morning and evening milkings.

We rarely had problems getting the cows in the barn and into their assigned stanchions because they were always eager to be milked at milking times. Every morning and evening at the appointed times, the cows usually collected at the barn door waiting patiently to enter. Their allotted grain was always placed in front of their stanchions before the barn doors were opened at milking times, and they were usually anxious to find their meals. The biggest distraction we encountered were warm early spring days when it was too pleasant for them to come indoors—especially when they were nearing the end of their periodic productive cycles. I remember one such day when one particular cow, which was going dry, was intent on staying outdoors in the barnyard. My father, a cousin, and I had managed to corner her near the entrance, but she refused to go through the open door. She just stood resolutely in front of the door, scanning us from side to side while she decided which way to bolt.

One thing you need to understand about early warm spring days in New Hampshire and Vermont is that frost, which drills up to three feet deep into the ground during the depths of winter, thaws gradually over time from the surface down. When warm weather arrives early, it can cause the top soil layers to thaw quickly while the deeper layers remain frozen solid. The remaining deep frost forms an impenetrable icy layer that traps the melted ice water at the surface, creating a thick, cold, waterlogged mud layer. When the cows gather and tramp around the barn entrance, the mud becomes especially mucky, in addition to being foul with manure. That night, my cousin apparently forgot about these conditions.

As we slowly closed in around the cow with our arms outstretched to each side to narrow the paths of escape, we trudged deeper into the smelly, soupy muck. For a few moments we stood still, waiting to see what the cow's next move would be. When she turned her head to bolt between my cousin and me, he instinctively lunged in my direction to close the gap. However, his boots had become stuck in the soggy muck, and he couldn't pull them loose. With no way to move his feet and his body shifting off balance, he gradually tipped over face first and flopped spread eagle into the stinky mud. Yes, he was covered from head to toe. Needless to say, the determined cow broke through, and his unfortunate landing became an image that will stay with me forever.

Each opposing row of stanchions in the barn stood before a roughly eight-foot-wide pad where the cows would stand while being milked. These pads sloped very slightly back into long gutters behind the cows where all of the manure and urine would eventually be collected. We would spread sawdust over the bare concrete pads where the cows stood to serve as relatively comfortable bedding, provide better footing, and absorb urine.

Along the ceiling above the exterior walkways between the gutters and the outer side walls of the barn was a monorail track that ran around three sides of the barn. Suspended from that track by wheeled pulleys and chains was a manure tub we could push and pull around the barn to shovel manure and waste into when we cleaned out the gutters. The track would lead the manure tub through a side door of the barn to an outside manure pit, where the manure would be piled until we could load it into the manure spreader and spread it over our fields as natural fertilizer.

Above the main floor of the barn was a full-length haymow where we stored both grain and hay. A large wooden grain bin was located above the central aisle of the barn with a dispenser chute that protruded down through the ceiling. We would park a two-bin wooden grain cart under the chute and fill it with grain, then walk the length of the central aisle scooping measured amounts of grain to each cow along the way. At the center and the opposing end of the central aisle were ceiling openings through which we could drop hay bales from the haymow to feed the cows.

The barn had three small room extensions along the sides. We used one as an indoor staging pen for recently born calves. There, we would feed them a milk formula until they were old enough to begin eating roughage. Then they would be moved into the heifer pen outside the barn.

The second accessory room was a small milk room that had been converted to storage. This room had been used to stage milk cans during each milking in the years prior to regulations that required all dairy farms to install refrigerated, stainless-steel, sanitary bulk storage tanks. In those earlier years, the milk from each cow was poured into milk cans until the end of the milking. Then they had to be immediately loaded onto a truck and delivered to the dairy in Springfield, VT. I have only vague memories from this milk handling practice, as it was discontinued when I was very young.

The third addition was the modern milk room where we installed the required bulk tank. It was too large to fit into the barn's original milk room. The tank had a refrigeration unit and a large, motor-driven paddle to stir the milk.

We couldn't afford to have a modern piping system to deliver the milk directly from the milking area into the bulk tank. We had individual vacuum-driven, stainless steel milking machines that we carried from cow to cow. Once a cow was done milking, we disconnected the machine, removed the lid and poured the milk into stainless steel pails. We then replaced the lid on the emptied milk can and moved it to the next cow. As the next cow began milking, we would carry the freshly filled pails into the milk room and pour the milk into an open strainer mounted on the top lid of the bulk tank. It was a time and labor-intensive process, but was much quicker than milking each cow by hand. That was something we had to do on many occasions when we lost electric power, because we couldn't afford to buy a generator to serve as a back-up power supply during an extended power failure.

Lifestyle Lost

On a dairy farm, the cows must be milked at regular intervals, regardless of whether or not the electric service is operating. If a power outage forced us to milk the cows by hand when it was dark outside, we would have to use kerosene lanterns hung from the manure tub track to see what we were doing. If the power was out for more than a few hours (and even less during the hottest summer days), we would have to dump all the milk stored in our bulk tank, because the dairy processor would not accept our milk if the bulk tank wasn't operating to keep the milk chilled to the proper temperature until the scheduled pick-up day. With all the hard work required to milk the cows, that was a frustrating, costly, and painful thing to do.

The milking barn was connected to the horse barn by a long ell that ran between them. It was nearly as long as the barn itself. The horse barn was a fine example of early American post and beam barn construction with massive mortise and tenon joints locked together with large, hand-hewn wooden pegs. It must have been one of the original buildings on the farm, and its advanced deterioration indicated that it had not been actively used for some time. It, too, had an upper floor haymow that connected to the milking barn along the ell. Unfortunately, this building had been out of use for many years before we bought the farm, and it was in such disrepair that it collapsed early in my childhood. When it collapsed, it took the connecting ell with it. As I recall, a number of the old beams were salvaged, but I can't remember what happened to them.

Another early building on our farm was called the corn shed. It was built using the same post and beam framing as the horse barn. The shed was built on stone masonry pillars, rather than a complete foundation wall. The floor area within the shed was limited, so we used it only as a storage building for tools and spare parts. The primary obstacle to other uses was the heavy wood-frame corn mill that occupied the middle of the floor. The device was used by prior generations to grind corn into meal to make cornmeal bread, pancakes, and other basic foods. I would estimate that it stood about four feet tall and measured about three feet in width on each side. It had a large, square wooden hopper on the top into which the shelled corn was loaded and a chute just above the base that dispensed the finely ground corn into some kind of bin or container. The inner workings were enclosed within the wooden sides of the mill, so you couldn't see them directly from the outside, but it was operated by a large, side-mounted, round metal crank with a wooden handle. The crank would operate the internal grinding mechanism (probably a grinding stone) to reduce the corn to ground meal as it gravity-fed from the hopper through the machine to the chute at the base.

The machine's relatively small size made it apparent that it was not used for commercial production, but to serve the needs of the immediate owners. I doubt that it was a fast or easy way to mill corn, any more than a butter churn or a hand-cranked ice cream maker is a fast or easy way to make butter or ice cream, but it was probably just as effective for its time. At least it helped previous owners provide for their needs in a way that contributed to their economic independence. Unfortunately, the corn mill had not been used for many years when we bought the farm, and we never experimented with it to see if it could still operate. It just remained in the shed until the building eventually collapsed and destroyed it.

Our farm complex also included a long chicken house (perhaps 40 feet in length). The previous owners apparently kept a large number of laying hens, but we used that building as a storage shed in which we kept spare lumber and all of our lawn/garden tools and equipment. Actually, as children, we often made use of the building as a make-shift "jungle-gym." Our father had placed an old rear tractor tire at the corner of the chicken house and filled it with sand for us to use as a sandbox. A tall purple lilac bush that grew about halfway down that side of the chicken house provided shade for the sandbox as well as a convenient climbing ladder for us to climb up onto the low side of the roof. We could spend an hour or more just climbing up onto the chicken house roof so we could jump off it into the sandbox. It seems silly to think about that today, but we had many hours of fun just doing that. That childhood fun and all the squatting I did to milk our cows may explain why my knees have become so worn and arthritic.

Three additional outbuildings completed the farm complex: a well-house that stood over a dug well last used by past generations of the previous owner, a long three-sided machine shed for the larger farm equipment we pulled with our tractor, and a two-car garage that we used as a work shop and to store our tractors. The garage was the newest of the outbuildings, and aside from the milking barn, (which still stands today) it was the last of the other six outbuildings to collapse from age, disrepair, and neglect. The multi-generational transition to a less self-reliant lifestyle gradually exacted its toll on the buildings and devices that supported a more colorful, traditional, and self-sufficient past.

****

Our life on the farm marked the period of transition between the former, more traditional and self-reliant farming lifestyle of the previous owners and the totally modern, non-farm use of the property today. We lived as self-sufficiently as we could, but we did make use of modern technology and machines. We simply never had the most current technology for our time.

The two tractors that my father bought with the farm were old, 1950-era John Deere model B tractors that had side-mounted flywheel drums on the engine. In my days, we used the flywheel on the tractors to power a belt-driven blower that forced corn silage up into the top of the barn silo. We always kept two working tractors over the years we worked the farm, but they were all older models that we bought second-hand. When we said we were getting a "new" tractor or piece of equipment, we really meant that it was new to us, not brand new. Even so, our scale of operation and income was never substantial enough to support a truly modern lifestyle, and we learned to make do with what we had.

Despite our use of tractors, some of our farm equipment and practices harkened back to an earlier era when the horse was the primary beast of burden. For example, our first plow and our corn planter were originally designed to be pulled by horses. The corn planter—a truly clever mechanical device—was built on a steel frame with metal wheels that angled inward to the center from both edges. The angle allowed the wheels to pack the soil back in on the planting trench carved by the twin metal planting spikes located at the front of the planter and aligned with each wheel. Corn seed was loaded into the two cylindrical seed containers with spring-loaded metal lids that were mounted on the top of the planter. As I recall, each seed container had about a two-to-three-gallon capacity, but I can't be sure after all these years. Everything looked a little bigger when I was young than it does today. We would mix some Stanley's Crow Repellant in with the seed, which was a foul-smelling black liquid tar that was mildly toxic to crows.

As the planter was pulled along, the rotating wheels would turn gears that operated the planting mechanism, while the planting spikes would dig into the soil and carve out the seed trenches. The mechanism released seeds from the bottom of the storage containers into tubes that dropped them at regular intervals into the planting trenches directly behind the planting spikes. The planter would make a clicking sound as it was pulled along, with each click indicating when it was depositing seeds into the planting trench. The operator rode on a metal bucket seat mounted between the wheels and operated a lever to disengage the planting mechanism and raise the planting spikes (and seed tubes) out of the soil when the planter reached the ends of the planting rows. Then, the planter could be turned around to start a new set of rows.

Because the planter's control lever had to be operated from the planter itself, planting corn became a two-person operation—one to drive the tractor and the other to operate the planter. If it had been pulled by a draft horse, as it was originally designed, it required only one operator. The planter could hold the reins of the horses with one hand and operate the control lever with the other. We didn't have any horses, so we had to use two people until my father bought a later model tractor with a three-point hitch and jury-rigged the planter to be lifted up at the end of each row by the tractor. Elements of our farm technology may have been somewhat outdated at the time, but they were still useful, and that was all that mattered to a family that preferred to live as free from the economic grip of the outside world as possible.

****

One of the biggest factors contributing to our simple and traditional farming lifestyle was our relative isolation from the surrounding modern society. My first trip to a big city was a school field trip to the Boston Museum of Science and New England Aquarium when I was about eleven or twelve years old. Although North Charlestown was only about 100 miles by Interstate highway from the modern city of Springfield, Massachusetts, we almost never traveled there. In fact, I was old enough to be driving on my first trip through downtown Springfield. We rarely traveled great distances, and our access to media from the outside world was very limited.

Lifestyle Lost

Throughout most of my childhood, the only commercial television station we could watch was the CBS network station (WCAX) from Burlington, Vermont. Burlington is Vermont's biggest city, but it cannot be called a major city by today's standards. The daily news broadcasts on that station were generally mundane and presented by a trio of long-time, venerable newscasters who were advancing in years even in my day—Richard Gallagher as the news anchorman, Stuart Hall as the weatherman, and Tony Adams as the sportscaster. Stuart Hall would sign off all of his ten-minute weather forecasts with a camera shot of a round, black wall clock and the words, "That's the weather, this is the time, now stay tuned for more news." He said that line exactly the same way so many times throughout my childhood that I can still hear his voice and inflections in my memory today. It never got any more exciting than that.

If we wanted to watch a program that was not broadcast on CBS during my youth, we had to visit a friend who had a rooftop rotary TV antenna. Cable television did not come to the small cities in our area until the late 1970s. I was sixteen-and-a-half years old before a new NBC station that we could receive began broadcasting out of Hanover, NH. It was around that time that we bought our first color TV. That was a significant technological advancement in our home for another reason. It was also the first solid state TV we had, which meant we no longer had to turn it on *before* a program began so the picture tube could have time to warm up.

Our local AM radio stations, WTSV in Claremont and WCFR in Springfield did not broadcast around the clock. They would both sign off around 10:00 PM every evening. Radio stations in New Hampshire and Vermont at that time had very weak signals, and the mountains made reception very difficult and spotty. The Claremont station would air a number of special programs that might sound strange to people today. I remember a program called "Candlelight and Music" that aired on Saturday evenings and played nothing but soft, romantic piano music. I also remember a weekend French-language radio program that opened to the song "Dominique" by the Singing Nuns every time it aired. We had a large French-Canadian population in New Hampshire that was drawn to jobs in the timber industry and textile mills. The state's largest daily newspaper, the Manchester Union Leader, included a section written exclusively in French. What few local FM stations we could receive merely repeated the same programming that was available on their

AM counterparts. FM radio was still in its infancy at that time, and the channels were even more difficult to receive than the AM stations.

At night, we could receive 50,000-watt AM radio stations from all across the country. We didn't receive them clearly, but I would play with the radio dial to see what stations I could find. I used to listen to St. Louis Cardinals baseball games on KMOX radio from St. Louis. I was an avid fan for years, and I still like to see them do well today. As a teenager, I would also listen nightly to the CBS Radio Mystery Theater on several of that network's affiliates, but mostly on WHAS from Louisville or WHAM from Rochester, NY. Their signals actually came in stronger than the CBS radio affiliate in Keene, NH (WKNE), which was only 35 miles south of where we lived. Once in a while on Saturday evenings, we would tune in the Jamboree USA on WWVA in Wheeling, WV while we were milking the cows. These nighttime radio stations were the best source of information on the outside world, aside from Walter Cronkite's nightly news broadcasts. That's the way it was.

While we did subscribe to the local daily newspaper out of Claremont, we had very few magazine subscriptions. The only regular subscriptions I can recall were Hoard's Dairyman and Yankee Magazine. These magazines were not a very broad window to the rest of the world. However, we did eventually inherit a lifetime subscription to Reader's Digest after my father's mother died. She had inherited it from her husband, who originally purchased the subscription long before he died. They must have been desperate to distribute their magazine, because it refused to expire even after my parents told them they didn't want it anymore. The last I knew, my mother had inherited it after my father died in 1984. Perhaps the greatest benefit I gained by not being part of my adoptive family anymore is the knowledge that I will not be next in line to receive it after my adoptive mother passes away. I guess that subscription is the only true gift in this world that keeps on giving.

Our family's social and recreational travels were limited primarily to extended family visits and occasional family reunions. We rarely went on long vacations for two obvious reasons. First, we had no money to afford lodging for a family of six (and in later years, seven), and second, the cows had to be milked twice daily. I can remember only two family vacation trips that lasted more than one day while we were actively farming. One was an overnight trip to York Beach, Maine, and the other was to attend a cousin's wedding in Saginaw, Michigan. Our trips to these locations were the first time in my life I had seen flat land. What additional recreational trips we made were limited to occasional day trips to one or more agricultural fairs or to the nearest lake beaches.

Our overall experiences and exposure kept us confined to the Upper Valley and central Lakes Region of New Hampshire, where my adoptive father grew up. As a result, we never felt closely connected to the more modern and urban areas of the country. Our limited contact and interaction with the outside world made it much easier to accept and appreciate the life we lived. We realized that life was different in the world outside our area, but the lifestyle we lived had a normal context within our confines and social circle. There was no reason to be jealous or envious of the outside life because it wasn't relevant to our isolated and closed society.

****

When you operate a farm, you do not get paid an hourly wage or even a salary for the work you do. We were periodically paid only when the product we produced was sold to the processing plant or an end consumer. Since our milk payment varied with the wholesale price of the milk and the amount of milk we produced, we were never certain what our income for any given shipment would be.   All of the expenses required for feed, fuel, fertilizer, seed, veterinary services, supplies, equipment or equipment repairs, and our own family's essential needs constituted an investment that had to be paid up front in *anticipation* of the sales check. The work we ended up doing on a daily basis wasn't paid labor, it was what we had to do to function and survive. If we received more money for the fruits of our labor than our cost of production, we considered ourselves lucky.

While many of our friends and acquaintances were not farmers, we all lived relatively simple, less technologically-dependent lifestyles that included elements of self-subsistence. For example, most people who lived in our community kept gardens and raised their own vegetables, even if they worked for one of the local industries. Some even raised small animals—from chickens and rabbits to goats and sheep—for food or sale. Most long-time and multi-generational residents did as much as they could with whatever land they owned to minimize their cost of living and make their lives affordable.

In our community, the Appalachian tradition of bartering was alive and *meaningful*. People often traded services or homemade items for the goods and services they needed. Some people would simply refer to it as "horse-trading." It really didn't matter what you chose to call it, bartering or trading things you had in abundance, could produce on your own, or no longer needed in exchange for things that you did need was an effective way of extending your purchasing power without using cash. It was so widespread in the area that the local radio stations would broadcast weekend swap and sell programs where residents could call in and offer what they had for cash or to exchange for something they needed.

I remember one day in the early 1970s, when a strangely dressed, lanky young man with a full beard, mustache, sideburns, and a heavy head of dark hair appeared at our door. I didn't understand it at that time, but we were meeting our first "back-to-the-land" free spirit from the hippie era. He had recently brought his family to Quaker City, a tiny hamlet in the town of Unity, NH, to join a small arts and crafts collective that emerged there. He was interested in finding certain types of wood and bark for his work that he noticed to be abundant on our land. Unfortunately, I'm not an expert on trees, and I've long since forgotten the specific species he was seeking. He wanted our permission to take some of our trees, but he had so little cash that he was concerned we'd turn him down. He probably received denials from other landowners he had previously approached, so he seemed very reluctant to ask.

As it turned out, his particular craft was making hand-hewn, straight back chairs with seats caned from a particular tree bark. My father listened intently to the man's explanation of his work. Although my father had a great appreciation of trees and fine wood products, I don't believe he was ever really trained in tree identification. While he could identify some of the common trees on our property, like oaks, maples, birches, and cherries, he really didn't seem to understand their specific properties well. He could sense the man's love for his work and decided to help him out. After the stranger finished his story, my father offered to let him take as much wood as he needed for a certain period of time (perhaps a season or two), as long as he removed the debris and made us a set of eight handcrafted chairs for our kitchen table. This was an extremely good idea, as we all spent so much time in the kitchen during the winter months that some comfortable new handcrafted chairs would be well appreciated by all.

The man agreed and returned within a few months with his promised delivery. The chairs had beautifully hand carved posts and slats that were joined with small wooden pegs. There was no metal used in them at all. All of the wooden members were meticulously sanded and lightly stained for a very rich appearance. The seats were all caned in bark, and they lasted for more than twenty years. I've never known such fine wood crafting since. They were unique heirloom pieces that we never could have afforded to buy.

A few years later, we were approached by a bee farmer from Maryland who wanted to know if he could set up some beehives for the season at the end of one of our fields. We worked out a deal where we were reimbursed in honey and received a large tin of honey annually for several years. We never again needed to buy it at the store during my childhood.

There were many other times when we would toddle off to some nearby farm under the formal pretense of visiting, but would end up with some informal exchange. If we asked where we were going on these impromptu trips, my father would often say, "We're going to see a man about a horse." While we might come away with something or an agreement to trade for something, it was never a horse. Whatever we got, it usually involved no exchange of cash, which extended our buying power for other critical needs.

This economic system and our network of like-minded people made it possible for us and our neighbors to live within our means and still serve our basic needs. As long as our basic needs were met and everyone else enjoyed a similar quality of life, there was no reason for us to feel deprived of a better life, even if it was all around us. I don't think that our fundamental goals in life—raise a family, provide a decent standard of living, and find enjoyment in life—were any different than for those who lived in the modern society, but our *expectations* of what it took to achieve those goals certainly were. Growing and producing much of what we needed, bartering to supplement our limited cash resources, and living within our means effectively allowed us to live on the edge of poverty without perceiving it that way. However, that is not the way that our modern, monetary wealth-based, technology-driven, urban society would view our basic lifestyle.

Since the scale of our operation was so small and our family was large, we lived on the margins most of the time and had little spare cash to spend on anything but the basic essentials that we could not provide for ourselves or obtain through bartering. This is how we learned the values and practices of self-reliant living even as we adapted to the use of more modern technologies and equipment.

****

A self-reliant family farm lifestyle is intimately choreographed throughout the year to the rhythms of the changing seasons and the fickle nuances of ever changing and inherently unpredictable weather conditions. Of course, the most basic chores, like those directly involved with milking, feeding, and caring for the cows, were a daily routine that had to be done seven days a week (with no paid weekends, sick days, vacations, or holidays off), but our overall work had multiple dimensions to it. Most of the other work involved in managing and operating the farm was driven by and tied to subtle changes in the seasons, and had to be choreographed with these changes precisely to ensure our eventual financial reward and ultimately, our survival.

This fundamental connection with the natural elements forces you to carefully observe and learn the patterns of change in the seasons, the shifting wind patterns and sky conditions that help foretell short term weather changes, and the long-term condition of the soil. As your ability to understand and read the environment around you grows, you become intimately aware of its importance to you and your survival. This is how the act of traditional farming (regardless of the scale at which it is practiced) gives you a deeper sense of closeness to and appreciation of the land and nature. It's what challenges you and nurtures you, all at the same time. Yet there is no greater sense of satisfaction or measure of independence than winning the battle with the elements. Let me explain how the changing seasons affected our patterns of work by leading you through a typical year on our farm, season by season.

The first hint of spring I can recall is the day that the air warms enough to have a fresh scent. During the depths of winter, the air in New Hampshire becomes so cold and dry that it lacks any real aroma. It only freezes your nostrils. However, as soon as the mercury first surges above the freezing mark, every gentle breeze carries with it the first fresh smell of spring. It's almost as though the air carries with it the very essence of life renewed from its winter home deep in the south to reawaken the land and plants.

Although the first scent of spring would arrive sometime around the vernal equinox, we knew that the leaves would not return to the trees until the lilacs were ready to bloom in May. Spring was a long and unforgiving season, filled with hope when the first promising patches of bare ground appeared in late March or early April only to be cruelly dashed a week later with a foot or more of snow from the final big snowstorm of the season.

Despite the climatic war that was being waged outside our door, spring was the time when life began to stir on the farm and preparations were made for the coming growing season. Even before the snow completely melted, the equipment had to be checked and serviced, essential spring supplies (and seeds) had to be purchased, and minor building repairs—which had been postponed out of respect for the brutal winter cold—were quickly completed. There was a renewed sense of urgency and anticipation to life that made it exciting and reminded you that you had almost survived the long winter.

One of the simple pleasures we would indulge to celebrate the approaching spring was a trip to a local sugarhouse for a taste of the season's fresh maple syrup. The sap would begin to run into the sugar maple trees in the first warm days in March. The trees would be tapped with metal spouts, and five-gallon sheet metal buckets bearing matching protective lids would be hung from the taps to collect the sap that slowly dripped from each spout. Since the sap runs during a time when the maple grove or forest is still covered in a blanket of snow, the sap was collected from the buckets using either a horse-drawn sledge (a small flatbed sleigh) or a wagon bearing a tank, tub, or barrels on it. The sap was then delivered to the sugarhouse where it was transferred into a wood or oil-fired evaporator that gradually boiled the water out of the sap, producing maple syrup. By the end of my childhood, this traditional sap collecting process was being replaced by long, flexible tubing lines that ran from tree tap to tree tap throughout the grove, which fed the sap directly to a collection tank or the sugarhouse.

The thrill of getting out of the house after a long, cold winter and into a warm, steam-bathed sugarhouse was almost irresistible. In addition to the embracing warmth you received from the intense heat and steam rising out of the wood-fired evaporator, you were enticed into the building by a pleasing, sweet maple scent that heightened your anticipation of the even sweeter taste to come. It was truly the first complete sensory treat of the season. While we couldn't go every season, we certainly went as often as our meager finances would allow.

During my childhood, the local sugarhouses offered free samples in tiny paper cups that held little more than a teaspoon of syrup each. We would compete to be the first to drink our free taste of nature's initial nourishing gift of the season. However, I don't know if they still do so today. Now that we live in West Virginia, we travel annually to a sugar camp (as they are affectionately called here) in Doe Hill, Virginia to enjoy that ritualistic experience once again. The local sugar camps closest to our Pendleton County retirement property offer no free samples.

If we were lucky, our next treat would be a cup of sugar on snow. This was a simple cup of shaved ice with a small ladle of maple syrup poured over it. The syrup would quickly congeal upon contact with the ice into a sticky paste, and we would peel it off the ice and eat it with a fork. Before leaving, we would get our gallon can of pure maple syrup for the year. Maple syrup and honey were sometimes used in our community as homemade cooking sweeteners to substitute for store-bought sugar. Many traditional recipes were made with maple syrup. That trip, with all the sights, smells, tastes, sounds, and reassuring warmth was always the perfect cure for cabin fever.

The next typical early spring activity was to begin planting vegetable seeds for the garden. We couldn't actually plant them in the garden, because the ground was still covered with snow and frozen solid by a deep layer of frost. We would plant the seeds in Dixie Cups or starter pots and place them in south-facing windows or under ultraviolet lamps to sprout plants that required a longer or earlier growing season than we would typically receive. It was cheaper to buy the seeds and grow them yourself than to buy potted vegetable plants, and starting the seeds early gave us a better chance of getting a bigger and longer harvest.

Although the calendar insists that spring begins in the third week of March, we would not firmly sense its arrival until the snow cover melted away in April. This was the start of the muddy season, which would last until the ground frost had completely relinquished its tenacious grip on the deepest layers of soil sometime in early May. This period in time was marked by the most fickle and indecisive weather of the season. Conditions could range from a full retreat into a blustery winter storm—to dank, misty, primeval days when the valleys and bare forests were soaked in dense fogbanks—to triumphantly reassuring sunny, warm spells when the air was thick with the aroma of awakening life, and color erupted from the landscape in the form of crocuses, daffodils, and dandelions. The resurrection of life was further affirmed by the sounds of awakening wildlife that emanated from the woods, heralded most prominently by the raucous twilight serenades of the spring peepers from the ponds across the road from our house. These sensory cues marked the true transition from winter to spring and set into motion the most intensive seasonal farming labors.

As soon as the snow and frost melted, we would begin plowing the garden and fields to prepare them for the summer crops. Our garden was very large by most standards and measured at least 150 feet long by 75 feet wide. Once the garden soil was broken up by the plow, we would break it up further and smooth it out with a harrow. Planting the garden was done by hand using a hoe. We would also lay down sheets of black plastic over the areas where we planted tomatoes to help keep the soil as warm as possible and to minimize weeds. Since weeds would typically become our most prolific garden crop, weeding the garden was a constant chore throughout the summer months.

The garden would eventually provide most of our summer vegetable needs. We would typically grow sweet corn, peas, potatoes, tomatoes, various squashes (including pumpkins), cabbage, Swiss chard, lettuce, spinach, carrots, cucumbers, turnips and/or parsnips (which I despised), peppers, yellow onions, and at least three varieties of beans. We also grew assorted herbs or specialty plants in smaller quantities, like horseradish, basil, oregano, catnip, and rhubarb. What produce we could not eat during the summer was sold to workers commuting to and from the nearby industries up the road from our house or dutifully canned in the fall and stored for the winter in our cool, dank cellar.

In addition to growing most of our own vegetables, we were also able to provide a good amount of our own meat. As children, we weren't told about this, but much of our fresh meat came from the cows that died or were simply too old to milk. Some of our male calves were also slaughtered for veal. The animals were taken to a local butcher shop in Claremont, which would prepare the meat for us. I don't know if we paid for this service, but it is quite possible that our pay was a percentage of the meat (yet another dimension of the Appalachian barter system). Our parents never discussed how we got our meat because we were so attached to our cows (especially one of my younger sisters who was always eager to work on the farm). Of course, we should have figured out that this was happening long ago, but we really didn't think about the fact that we very rarely had to bury our cows.

Preparing the fields for spring planting season would also trigger one of the most tedious and backbreaking farming jobs—rock picking, as we called it. One thing that must be understood about the soils in New Hampshire, Vermont, and West Virginia is that no matter how well they grow crops, they always seem to grow rocks better. When my wife and I bought our retirement property in West Virginia and started planting apple trees on it, we quickly realized that we had paid for the rocks and got the land for free. I'm sure my parents felt the same way about our New Hampshire farm.

Fortunately for us, most of our cultivated land was right along the river and consisted of a fine silty loam that had very few rocks. However, as you moved away from the river (even to the other side of the highway), the conditions rapidly changed. Rock picking was a ritual triggered by plowing. As the plow turned the soil, it would inevitably turn up rocks and stones, some of which could easily weigh twenty pounds or more. Great care had to be taken with the plow not to damage the blade on large rocks that were either partially or completely buried. After the soil had been broken and turned, the rocks had to be removed before we could harrow the field.

As you might expect, this meant combing through the field following the tractor and a flat-bed trailer to pick up the rocks by hand and pile them on the trailer. When the field was cleared of rocks or the trailer was full (whichever came first), the rocks were taken to the edge of the field and piled loosely along the property line. New England is famous for its rustic stone walls, but many of the walls that look like jumbled piles were created over time by farmers picking rocks.

The work was hard enough, but the frosty air of early spring and even colder, damp soil that you had to dig them out of made the task even more uncomfortable. Perhaps the worst aspect of it was that it was the first heavy labor of the season following a long winter with less physical activity. It didn't take long under those conditions to work up a good backache. Fortunately, we didn't have to do this every season, and the need became less frequent after the land had been worked over for a few years.

Spring was also the season for fencing. To a farmer, fencing involves a roll of barbed wire or wooden rails, not a sword. After a heavy snow season that often brought down large limbs and trees, the fences around our fields and pastures had to be repaired. The fencing around our cattle pens and pastures typically consisted of either two strands of electric fence or a top strand of electric fence and two lower strands of barbed wire. Electric fencing required a ceramic insulator that was nailed to the post, while barbed wire was nailed to the post using staples, which essentially were U-shaped nails with points on both ends. Fencing work involved walking or driving along every fence line and fixing all of the downed or broken sections. When replacing or expanding barbed wire fences, a wire stretcher had to be used to make sure the fence was as taut as possible before it was nailed to the post. Occasionally, wooden fence posts would have to be replaced.

As the weather continued to warm and spring peacefully melted into summer (sometime in mid-to-late-May), planting season would begin. This is when we would plant corn, using our old, reliable horse-drawn corn planter that I described earlier. Every so often we also had to spread more fertilizer and/or alfalfa and timothy grass seed on our hayfields, just to keep them producing an efficient yield of hay. This annual planting work was made easier and more efficient because we used a tractor. It was far different for earlier generations that had to rely on horses or oxen as the primary beasts of burden for plowing and planting work.

Those farmers who raised sheep and goats would have another spring task to perform. Although we didn't raise any sheep or goats on our farm, we did help a little old lady from our community shear the winter coat of wool from the two or three sheep she raised. She would use the wool to make yarn with her spinning wheel. Her name was Dora Dean, and she lived just over a half mile up the road from our farm. She was a 75-85-year-old unmarried woman who lived one of the most primitive and self-sufficient lives in our area.

Dora's house was very old and had not been upgraded since it was built—probably in the late 1800s. I never asked her when it was built. It had weathered clapboard siding, a stone foundation wall, and a packed dirt floor that was slightly higher than the outside ground level, but just one stone layer below the top of the foundation and the bottom sills of the exterior walls. To the best of my memory, her house had only one separate room (her bedroom) and a central stone fireplace that had been closed in with an antique wood-fired cookstove installed in front of it. That may have been the only improvement that was ever made to the house since it was built. Her bathroom was an outhouse located behind the house from the highway. The sink within the house had a hand-operated water pump connected to a well just outside the house. She had no electric service in her house, and her sole entertainment was a battery-operated radio and the books she may have read by lantern. She kept a large garden in her back yard and stored canned vegetables in a cold shed that was partly below grade. It may have also been built into an earthen bank—I just can't remember clearly. All of her furniture was made of wood, and she slept on an old-fashioned rope bed with a straw-filled mattress and hand-made quilts for bedding.

Dora would shuffle down the highway to our house two or three times a week to scoop out a couple quarts of milk from our bulk tank. She was always dressed in a homespun dress, heavy ankle shoes laced tightly, and either a kerchief or bonnet (depending on the weather conditions) over her wavy silver hair. She would always bring one of her goats with her to carry her milk bottles, because she had a severely hunched back from a bad case of osteoporosis. She would tie the milk bottles together with a braided rope and strap them securely over the goat's back. Her condition never slowed her down, and she would always explain with a hearty laugh that her posture resulted from too many years of pulling weeds that always fought back. I don't believe that we told her what to pay for our milk, but she would always dig a couple of coins out of her cloth coin purse and give them to us for the privilege. She was so stubbornly independent that it was always better to take what she offered than to convince her not to bother.

Despite the extremely primitive living conditions that surrounded her and the depth of her poverty, we never knew her to be unhappy with her life. I know this because, as young children, our parents would pay her to baby sit us on the rare occasions they had to take care of business in town. Sometimes, she would come to our house and, if the weather was bad, we would stay at her house. When she stayed with us, we rarely watched television. She would captivate us with ghost stories and tales about her childhood. She was descended from a long line of story-tellers, so she knew just how to tell them and make them captivating. I only wish I could remember some of them, but all I can recall are bits and pieces.

Dora was always in a good mood and never complained about her situation. Her self-confidence was evident by her frequent, cheery smiles, despite the fact that she had lost all but a few of her teeth. She passed away shortly after I moved on to college, and my mother told me that, shortly after her death, the town declared her house to be unfit and had it demolished. That was the sad and unceremonious end to the life of a very pleasant, strong, and resolutely independent woman. Although her life was hard, a fact that was clearly reflected in her grizzled and worn face, she was a truly engaging and beautiful person. I, for one, will never forget her.

As summer matured, our activity on the farm built to a determined pace. We had to keep up with the crops and begin preparations for the approaching fall harvest and winter. The most frantic summer activity was haying. First the hay was cut with a side-bar mower. It was allowed to dry for a day or two before we raked it into windrows using a side-delivery rake. The device had two large metal disks (one on each side of the implement) connected along the outer edges by several shafts that angled back from the front of the rake. Along each shaft was a row of long metal tines that swept just above the level of the ground as the disks rotated. A gear assembly attached directly to and driven by the rake's tire axle rotated the disks and connecting tine-shafts counter-clockwise (relative to the wheels) as it was pulled around the field. This action allowed the tines on each rotating shaft to capture the mowed grass and gradually roll it into a windrow at the far side of the rake. After another day or two of drying in the sun and wind, we would bring in a hay-baler that would pick up the windrows of hay and compress and bind them into rectangular bales that would litter the field.

Since this process required several continuous days of dry, sunny weather, which—if you know New England weather very well—is almost impossible to expect, we were always in a rush to get it picked up and loaded into our barn before the next rain. This meant walking around the field beside a tractor and a flatbed trailer (and/or a pick-up truck, if necessary), picking up the bales by hand and tossing them onto the wagon to be stacked. After years of practice, I could toss a bale of hay at least ten feet off the ground onto the top of the load and place it right where it needed to be stacked. The work was made more challenging if it rained on the hay before it could be loaded and increased the dead weight of each bale from roughly 30 pounds to as much as 50 pounds. It was hard enough to load hay in the intense summer sun, but it was harder still to load it faster in the rain. If you have watched this being done while driving in the country, be thankful you are a tourist.

After the wagon was loaded with hay, it was taken to the barn and unloaded onto a series of hay elevators that would deliver the bales up to the haymow. We would then toss the bales from person to person until they were stacked. If loading the hay onto the wagon was hard, stacking them in the confines of the barn was pure torture. First of all, the heat within the haymow was intense, with the summer sun beating down on the upper floor of the barn that was insulated by hay. In addition to the heat, tossing and stacking the hay produced a dense fog of chaff in the air that would stick to the sweat on your skin and choke you as you gasped for breath in the stifling heat.

After each load was stacked, we were more than ready to be hosed down by a fire truck. However, we didn't own a fire truck, and the work was rarely done after just one load. Consequently, the most relief you could get was a tall glass of ice-cold Kool-Aid or lemonade. Then, it was back to the field for the next load. When we were finally done for the day, we would run across the highway to the pond and jump in for an hour or so before supper. Bear in mind that done is a relative term on a farm. We hayed several fields, and each field would produce at least two and perhaps three cuttings of hay during a summer season. It was difficult to understand why, at the end of the season, the pond was not completely covered by a thin layer of floating hay chaff.

Cutting firewood was another task that had to be started in early spring or summer to make sure the wood would be dry enough to burn in the winter. We would start with any trees that might have fallen in the winter or early spring. The wood first had to be cut into stove length (roughly sixteen inches) segments with a chain saw and then split by hand throughout the summer and fall months using an ax or a few wedges and a sledgehammer. We typically used between six and eight cords of wood in an average winter. A cord of wood is a stack that is four feet tall by four feet wide by eight feet long (or roughly 128 cubic feet). Where I will be retiring in Pendleton County, WV, I believe we should be able to get by with about two-to-three cords of firewood in a typical winter. Such is the difference in severity and duration between New Hampshire and West Virginia winters.

If, with all our other warm weather chores, we didn't have enough time to cut our own wood, we would obtain it from someone else. Given the amount of wood we needed, the wood splitting work would often continue into the winter.

Sometime in early September, the skies would turn dark and gray and the first strong, foreboding winds of fall would sweep down from the mountains. By the first day of fall, the nighttime temperatures would tumble into the upper 30s and the leaves on the trees would begin to assume their brilliant shades of gold, bronze, and crimson. This is the time of the Harvest Moon, the full moon closest to the fall equinox, when the rising orb at sunset adds an extra hour to the dwindling evening twilight so that farmers can work longer to bring in the harvest. This is the time on our farm when our work would reach a truly frantic fever pitch.

Lifestyle Lost

In this time of the year, our primary focus would turn to the garden and the cornfields. Whatever summer vegetables we didn't eat or sell during the summer months had to be quickly harvested before the first hard freeze, which typically occurred in mid-to-late September. This excess food would be canned for the winter, which meant that our kitchen would be transformed into a full-scale food processing plant. Ball canning jars, glass lids, and rubber seals were cleaned and sterilized. Vegetables were rinsed and chopped up. Once the canning jars were filled, they were placed in a pressure cooker to be sealed. Then the preserved bounty was stored on shelves in the cool cellar.

In the cornfields, an armada of heavy equipment was staged to harvest the corn. Our tractor was connected to a corn chopper that would digest two rows of cornstalks at a time into silage that was blown into the back of a revolving fleet of staged trucks. As one truck would deliver a load to the farm for storage, a second empty truck would take its place. The whole process kept moving, almost non-stop, to ensure that the corn was harvested as quickly and efficiently as possible.

In my early years, our corn silage was stored in the silo that was attached to a corner of the milking barn. In front of the silo, we kept a corn blower to load the corn into the top of the silo. The device consisted of a long trough with a feed auger in the bed. Corn silage would be off-loaded or dumped into the trough and the rotating auger would carry it along to the blower at the base of the long chute that extended up the side of the silo and into an opening in the domed roof. The blower used a series of swiftly rotating metal paddles to blow the corn from the end of the auger up the chute and into the silo to fill it. The device had a metal flywheel on the opposite side of the blower from the trough. This flywheel would be connected to the flywheel on one of our tractors using a long, wide leather belt. The tractor's engine would rotate the flywheel on the corn blower and operate a series of gears and axles that drove the auger and the blower simultaneously.

Over the years, the silo aged and developed a list. At that point, it became too dangerous to use for storing corn silage, so we created a bunker in which to pile the corn and covered it with black plastic and worn-out truck tires to hold it in place. The silo, like most of the other buildings on our farm, eventually collapsed and was removed.

Another early fall ritual met with great anticipation was apple picking. Although we did not grow any apple trees, we did routinely visit a small orchard within a half mile of our house that was located immediately behind Farwell School. This orchard specialized in Macintosh apples, which was the sweetest local variety and my personal favorite. I still feel they make the best apple pies, which was one of my mother's and grandmother's real specialties.

A trip to the orchard meant that we children could climb the apple trees and pick a bushel of apples. This dangerous activity was conducted in the time just before civil law suits and liability waiver forms were invented. Some of the apples would be eaten raw, but most were transformed into apple pie filling, applesauce, and apple jelly.

On a few occasions during my childhood, we visited a local cider mill to buy fresh apple cider and apple juice. I don't recall exactly where it was located, but it was a traditional mill powered by a water wheel. The wheel operated the apple mill in the center of the building, which consisted of a crusher at the top and a press at the bottom. The crushed apples would be deposited into the press and the press would compress the apples into a fine screen that filtered out the juice from the seeds, stems, and skins. The result was fresh apple juice that could be fermented lightly into cider or, after a somewhat longer aging process, into hard cider or "applejack," which was a type of apple brandy. We weren't in the market for alcohol, so we would just obtain our cider and leave. Some of the cider we obtained would be allowed to age and ferment into apple vinegar.

After the peak of fall foliage season had come and gone came the raking of leaves. We had a large lawn and a lot of trees, so we had a lot of leaves to rake up. The occasional strong, gusty winds of late October and early November made this work a constant challenge. We often spent as much time chasing the leaves in the wind as we did raking them into piles. As I discussed earlier, we would rake the leaves into lawn and leaf garbage bags, tie them up, and stack them around the foundation walls of our house to serve as insulation. We would also work to seal up the windows in the house and barn for the winter.

Of course, the first November snowfall would send armies of people into the woods to hunt. Many people in our area would supplement their diets by hunting and fishing. We were not among them. Given the generally depleted deer herd in our area in those years and our farming demands, we simply couldn't invest the time that might be needed to hunt for additional meat (over and above what we obtained from our slaughtered cows). We did occasionally fish in the Connecticut River or Ox Brook, but our catch was used to stock our ponds, not to eat (because the river was determined to be contaminated with PCBs). Although popular, hunting was a dying tradition in New Hampshire during my childhood. I was surprised to learn that it is alive and well in West Virginia. I don't know if I can handle dressing a deer, but I might be tempted to try it someday early in my retirement. It is certainly a good way to obtain meat for the winter.

If the snow wasn't too deep after Thanksgiving, my mother would make her only major trip into the woods to clip and collect Hemlock tree boughs and red berries. These sprigs were twisted to a round wire ring using wire bands to create Christmas wreaths that would be hung from our doors. Christmas was the biggest holiday in our family, and every effort was made to decorate the house for it. Bough collecting had to be done quickly. The first couple of weeks in December would usually bring the season's first heavy snowfall (ten inches or more), which covered the ground with a blanket of white that would gradually build up and remain in place continuously until the first major thaw in March.

As the winter season tightened its frosty grip, work on the farm diminished to the daily routines that carried us throughout the year. The standard winter chores were only made more unpleasant by the bitter cold, biting winds, and deep snowdrifts. The only new chore demanded by the season was snow shoveling and plowing. Aside from Christmas, winter was a long, hard season that few were eager to embrace. A good portion of our time would be spent watching it from the kitchen and feeding the fervent, inexhaustible appetite of the woodstove.

This, in a nutshell, illustrates how our daily lives and work responsibilities were influenced by the changing seasons. Farming is not an easy life, and severe weather conditions (drought, floods, storms, and sudden cold snaps) could affect your success and your ability to survive. You lived with the lingering fear of a prolonged illness or a debilitating injury that could leave you seriously behind in your work. A successful harvest was never assured. You had to follow the seasonal weather patterns as closely as you could and hope that Mother Nature and good fortune would appreciate, respect, and reward your efforts. After all, your very life depended on it. However, you could always appreciate the knowledge that the battle for survival was reduced to you and nature. You were beholding to nothing else. Success, despite the odds, was the pride you gained from a life of true independence.

****

Although we lived our lives as self-sufficiently as we could, we could never forget or ignore that we were part of a larger community. Our extended family, friends, and acquaintances were all part of the larger supporting institution that made North Charlestown a true community. These social bonds were supported and validated by the central institutions in the community—the church and Farwell School.

However, this one area marks a subtle, but distinct cultural difference between the traditional Appalachian societies of northern New England and West Virginia. In West Virginia, the church is the primary social institution outside the family that binds communities together. While most multi-generational New Englanders hold deep religious beliefs and traditions, they do not share them as openly or as fervently as their mountain brethren to the southwest. Their religious beliefs are held and practiced privately within each family.

That is not to say that the church is not an important social institution. Most of the people in my community attended the North Charlestown Methodist Church. However, the roots of the traditional community go back in time to the original social impetus for the American colonies—the intense religious persecutions of small and emerging religious groups by the powerful, politically-connected, established churches of northern Europe. The people who first settled New England were religious refugees as much as they were economic refugees. They came with many other new and reformist religious sects, such as the Puritans and Quakers (which were *not* limited to Pennsylvania). These initial basic groups quickly diversified into other sects, including the Shakers and even the Mormons, who actually originated in Vermont in the early 1800s and migrated west to Utah.

With such initial and growing diversity in religious beliefs among a people so highly concentrated in a small geographic area, the need to exercise religious restraint and tolerance emerged out of necessity as an important core value. The near religious implosion triggered by the Salem witch trials in the late 1600s only reinforced the need for religious restraint. Consequently, people learned that their communities did not arise from a specific church or one set of shared beliefs, but through the acceptance and peaceful (harmonious) co-existence of a wide range of religious beliefs and practices.

Over time, New Englanders learned to tolerate different religious beliefs and to treat their own religious values as personal or private choices that were shared formally and with great restraint only within the confines of the church or their own families. New Englanders are often characterized as very private people, and religion is the primary motivating factor driving that distinctive characteristic. I, too, was influenced by that traditional value, and I do not practice my personal beliefs openly, nor do I preach them to others. I have an intense interest in the differences and common themes in many religious beliefs, but I do not broadcast or advertise my own. It's just the way I am.

Our own family's involvement in the North Charlestown Methodist Church was actually quite limited. Our father was not a frequent church-goer, in large part because the demands of farming work aren't always conducive to observing the Sabbath as a day of rest. New England Yankees are a hardy and determined sort that cherishes a dedication to hard work as another core value. While my father considered himself to be a faithful man, he could not simply abandon one core value for another. Our family attended church routinely when we were young, but gradually withdrew over time as we aged and the burdens of maintaining the farm grew.

What I remember most vividly about the local church was the church bell, which tolled proudly every Sunday morning before the services began. The children of the church would take turns ringing the heavy bell, and you could hear the differences in the strength and volume of the tolls. Actually, the bell was so heavy that it would lift me off the floor when I was given the opportunity to ring it in my early childhood years. Even after we stopped attending the church regularly, we could hear the bell toll out on Sunday morning from our farm roughly half a mile away. In fact, I can remember only one time during my childhood that I heard the church bell toll at any other time or on any other day. That occurred when I was awakened early from sleep on October 21, 1975 by the raucous clanging of the bell— even louder than I had ever heard it before. How can I be certain of that specific date? Because all the church bells in Charlestown rang that night after the town's native son, Carlton Fisk, hit a dramatic solo home run in the bottom of the 12th inning to give the Boston Red Sox a 7-6 win over the Cincinnati Reds in the 6th game of the 1975 World Series.

My wife and I were pleasantly surprised when we discovered, while working to build our retirement home, that we could hear the steeple bell of Wilson Chapel in Brushy Run, WV tolling around 10:30 AM on most Sunday mornings. After just a few Sundays, I quickly learned that the children of that church were taking turns ringing the bell, just as they had done where I grew up. It is quite easy to hear the same varying intensities in strength and volume that was all too familiar from my childhood in North Charlestown. We now listen intently at that time every Sunday morning when we are working on our house to enjoy that pleasant, reassuring, and reaffirming sound.

However, the primary social institution in North Charlestown was not the Methodist Church. It was the Farwell School. Its story and my experiences in it remain some of the strongest memories that I have from my childhood.

The importance of the school to our community stems from its rather unique form of administration. Prior to the construction of Farwell School, the children of North Charlestown attended one of four different one-room school houses that were scattered around the community. The community's wealthy benefactor, Jesse Farwell, donated the funds needed to build a central school in the village to replace the previous small one-room schools. The deed of trust that transferred the school to the community established a board of five trustees (made up of North Charlestown citizens) to oversee, administer, and maintain the school. The former separate school districts were combined and the taxes that supported the previous schools were transferred to the new consolidated school under the financial administration of the board of trustees.

This form of administration gave the school a special status within the community. Over the years, parents from across the community would volunteer their time (and materials) to work on the school during the summer recesses and make the necessary repairs and improvements. Eventually, the North Charlestown Mother's Club was organized and became the primary vehicle to marshal and organize volunteer labor. The school had become the focal point of the community, and its impact touched virtually every family.

This arrangement worked well for at least 75 years, until Charlestown became one of five adjoining towns to organize the Fall Mountain Regional School District in 1965. The district built a new central high school to be shared by all five towns and, in doing so, altered the former town taxing districts and established a new board of education comprised of members representing the various communities. These changes effectively transferred Farwell School's primary source of funding from the board of trustees to the regional school district and gave the district's regional board of education control of the school.

Farwell School had served all of the community's students from first through ninth grade. As in most rural schools, students in multiple grades were taught in the school's two classrooms. By the time that the regional district was formed, only six grades remained in the school. Beginning in seventh grade, students from North Charlestown were transferred to the town's former high school in the main village.

Once the board of education took administrative control of Farwell School, it determined that the school was overcrowded and transferred grades five and six away to the old Charlestown High School, which was reorganized as an elementary school that would feed into the new regional high school. In 1967, the regional school board considered a petition to close Farwell School. The North Charlestown community protested and the petition failed. However, by the time I began first grade at the school in 1968, the regional school board had decided to transfer the fourth grade away. The North Charlestown community was experiencing its loss of control over the school and the gradual erosion of its student body. This was not a good way to win the community's support for the new regional school district.

The issue of Farwell School's fate under the regional district came to a head in 1970, when the regional school board unexpectedly voted to close it. Discord over divided control of the school between the regional district and the board of trustees had left the school in desperate need of maintenance for a number of years. The trustees had lost their control of the tax proceeds and could not afford to maintain the school after it fell under the regional district's authority. Likewise, the regional district felt that it could not effectively administer a school that the board of trustees owned. The inevitable battle over the ultimate fate of the school had been waged, and the citizens of North Charlestown responded aggressively. From the community's perspective, it was a fight to preserve its own identity as a distinct community against a large outside bureaucracy that was controlled by other towns.

After a bitter debate, an agreement was reached. The regional school district agreed to rent Farwell School from the board of trustees and, in turn, the trustees agreed to resume maintenance responsibilities. The regional district agreed to pay the teachers' salaries, and the board of trustees was allowed to interview the teachers during the hiring process.

Once this agreement was reached, the trustees organized another volunteer army of citizens in the summer of 1970, led by the Mother's Club, to undertake extensive and long overdue repair work. Our family pitched in to help. The school's roofing was replaced, the interiors were repainted, the hardwood floors were refinished, electrical wiring was replaced, windows were repaired, and the school was restored to its former glory. The community remained dedicated to the school, and it is still in use today. In fact, a new building was built in a portion of the apple orchard behind it and the combined school campus now accommodates grades 1-6. Farwell School's survival and rejuvenation stand as a testament to the determined resistance of a small community against outside control and influence—and to the core value of self-reliance shared by the people it served.

Lifestyle Lost

When I began attending Farwell School for first grade in 1968, Mrs. Leahy and Mrs. Champney were the two teachers. Both were elderly ladies at the time and may have been born in the late 1800s. First grade was taught by Mrs. Leahy and third grade was taught by Mrs. Champney. After the fourth grade class was relocated in the middle of that school year, the second grade was divided in two between the two teachers. I ended up being assigned to Mrs. Champney for both second and third grades.

My first grade teacher was from a very different era. Mrs. Leahy informed us all very early in the school year that we were expected to behave and give her our undivided attention. She warned us that if we misbehaved, we could expect to be taken out back to the shed behind the school and treated to "the switch," which she kept in her closet. I don't ever recall seeing the switch used, but I do remember a battle that she had in the classroom with an unruly student who was bigger and taller than anyone else in our class. His name was Michael, and he had his own idea of what he needed to learn and what he didn't.

One day when Mrs. Leahy said we were going to study one of those subjects that Michael had decided that he didn't need to learn, he protested by emptying the books out of his desk and throwing them to the front of the classroom. Mrs. Leahy thundered over to his desk, grabbed Michael by the ear (and perhaps some of his curly black hair), and yanked him out of his chair and down onto the floor. Michael didn't appreciate her actions and a scuffle ensued that sent a number of the students (and some of the surrounding desks and chairs) towards the sides of the classroom. Michael was a big kid for his age, but having been taken down to his knees, Mrs. Leahy knew she had a fighting chance to control him. Every time Michael would try to regain his balance to slug her, she would slap him in the head or kick him and send him back down to the floor.

Once it was apparent that the battle would end in a stalemate, calm gradually ensued, and Michael was allowed to stand up. After that contest, Michael learned a new level of respect for her, and I don't ever recall seeing him seek a rematch. In fact, he spent the rest of that day sitting alone in the hallway between the two classrooms. At some point during my tenure at the school, his family moved away to Arizona, and that was the last I saw of him.

I once had my own moment of confrontation with Mrs. Leahy, although it was more of a reaction than a deliberate act. One of the first things we were taught in first grade was how to write our ABC's. At that time, it was called penmanship. Mrs. Leahy would pass out papers with green print on them. These forms would have multiple sets of three parallel lines (the middle line was dashed, while the top and bottom lines were solid) that ran the width of the paper. The top set of lines had one letter of the alphabet printed repeatedly across it in both capital and lower-case form. We were instructed to trace the letters in the top row using a big, round, black pencil and then write it on our own in the remaining sets of blank lines provided down the rest of the page. It sounds simple enough, but I had one small disability that Mrs. Leahy despised. I am left-handed.

Being from a much different era, Mrs. Leahy was of the impression that writing with, or for that matter using, your left hand was the "Devil's work." That's what she told me one time, and she spent the rest of the year determinedly trying to break me of that bad habit (as she referred to it). Whenever we were asked to do our penmanship work, she would patrol the aisles with a wooden ruler in her hand to keep order and make sure we were focused on our work. One day, she came up behind me while I was breaking the law and using my left hand. I guess I didn't hear her coming, so I didn't have a good opportunity to cover up my infraction by switching hands. I had gotten pretty sneaky at doing this when I knew she was watching.

This time, she caught me unaware, and she swiftly slapped that ruler down across my knuckles, knocking the pencil out of my quivering hand. She didn't break the skin on my fingers, but I can remember clearly more than forty years later just how much it hurt. I screamed from the pain and startled everyone else in the classroom. As the pain quickly transformed to anger, I reacted by crumpling up the paper and throwing it all the way to the front of the classroom. I had never been one of Mrs. Leahy's problem children to that point, so I think my reaction surprised her just as much as the thought of her pending response scared me.

I guess she felt a little sorry for hitting me so hard, which might have been completely unintentional on her part. She didn't apologize, but I also didn't get slapped or treated to the dreaded switch. Since she couldn't bring herself to show any sympathy (that might diminish her control over the more unruly children), she simply directed me to pick up my pencil, sit up perfectly straight, and fold my hands on the desk until everyone was finished with the assignment. I felt quite lucky that day. I don't know if she ever caught me using my left hand after that, but she never hit me again with that trusty ruler.

I tried hard to learn how to write with my right hand that year. I managed to figure out how to do it, but it always felt unnatural to me, and my handwriting was never as good as it was when I used my left hand. When I advanced to second grade, I moved into Mrs. Champney's classroom. Once again, we had to do penmanship work, and my efforts at writing with my right hand produced somewhat sloppy work. As I recall, penmanship is the only subject where my grade dropped dramatically from one year to the next during my education at Farwell School. Eventually, I discovered that Mrs. Champney didn't care if I wrote with my left hand, and I gradually switched back. Even today, I write and eat with my left hand, but I throw, bowl, and bat right-handed. You figure it out. I guess the Devil succeeded in controlling only part of me.

Whether we liked it or not, school was not something we could avoid. Not only were our parents very strict about that point, but we children also believed that our grandmother was part of a grand parental conspiracy to prevent us from getting out of a day of school. When we felt too sick to attend school in those early years, our grandmother would often come to the house to administer traditional remedies—many of which were far worse to survive than the dreaded disease itself. We were occasionally given Caster oil, asafetida bags, and various herbal tea and special coffee drinks—including sassafras, catnip, and peppermint tea and something called brown bread coffee, which was intended to soothe an upset stomach. Where these bizarre ancient remedies originally came from, we were never sure. Nor would knowing have made them any easier to take. We were all quite certain that the *real* reason for administering them was to make sure we weren't playing sick. I drank so many of those old remedies as a child that they eventually cured me of any interest in drinking coffee or tea. Even today, I refuse to drink them. Just the smell of some coffees and teas can instantly remind me of being sick.

Despite the rather stern discipline of our teachers, the constant prodding from our parents, and the outdated, British textbooks we had to learn from (most of them were printed by London Press), I still feel we received our best education at Farwell School. Schooling was less of an *institutional* experience in those years and more of a *community* experience. Learning in a classroom that taught multiple grades was a real advantage. Our teachers would work with one grade on a subject, and then give us an assignment to work on quietly. Then they would instruct the other grade until they were given an assignment, and they could turn their attention back again to the other grade. You see, multi-tasking was actually practiced long before the twenty-first century.

This teaching system may sound inefficient or outmoded relative to the more formal and institutionalized teaching practices of today, but it was a real benefit to the students. I feel that it kept many students from falling behind. By hearing the instruction given to the older students, the younger students got a preview of what they would be learning in the next grade. That made it feel less scary to advance into the next grade and gave the quick-learners an opportunity to get a head start on the next year's instruction. On the other hand, the teachers would often allow the older students to help the younger students with a subject they didn't understand. This gave the older students a chance to reinforce what they had learned, just as it helped the younger students who were struggling to understand. Being taught a difficult subject by someone who had just learned it the year before and was closer to your own age felt less intimidating. I feel that this reciprocal training made it far easier for us to understand and retain what we learned.

Our curriculum also extended beyond the textbook and reinforced our attachment to and understanding of the area in which we lived. Mrs. Leahy and Mrs. Champney would occasionally tell us stories of the various legends and history of New Hampshire. I remember learning the sad story of "Nancy in the Snow."

Nancy was a young pioneer American girl who lived in Lancaster, NH, about 100 miles north of us on the Connecticut River. She was in love with and had agreed to marry a dashing young man who, without warning, disappeared and left her behind. Torn by her unyielding love for him, she set out on foot in the middle of the winter to find him. She headed south into the high peaks, bitter cold, and ferocious weather of the White Mountains. While struggling through Jefferson Notch, she lost one of her mittens, yet she struggled on with every ounce of dwindling energy. When her search party found it, they named the imposing peak that loomed over the site Mount Mitten—which is the name it still bears today. She eventually made her way south into Crawford Notch, where her dwindling strength could carry her no farther. The search party finally found her frozen body huddled peacefully in the shelter of a towering spruce tree along the Saco River. Nancy Mountain, Nancy Pond, and the hiking trail leading to them are all named for her.

We were told many old Indian legends (including the tales of Chief Chocorua, Hannah Dustin, and of course, local heroine Susannah Johnson). They also told us stories about German spies in New Hampshire during World War II who would climb to the summit of Mount Monadnock (near Keene) at night and signal messages to German submarines lurking in Massachusetts Bay. Many of these old stories I remember today. As children, we were all spellbound by the tales. But, most importantly, they built in us a strong connection to a shared heritage and to a culture that reflected how we lived.

Farwell School also sponsored and produced the biggest social event of the year in North Charlestown, the annual Christmas Pageant at the old theater in the Sugar River Grange Hall. Each November, the school children would practice songs and Christmas skits that each class would perform in the week before Christmas. The entire community would gather to watch the performance, which always ended with a visit by Santa Claus bearing a large bag of gifts and fruit for the kids. I also can vaguely recall one Christmas early in my childhood when I joined a small party of children that boarded a horse-drawn sleigh and traveled along a snow-packed gravel road to visit the homes of the most elderly shut-ins of our community and sing Christmas carols to them. It was and remains my one and only experience riding in a sleigh.

Lifestyle Lost

All of these activities, stories, events, and memories tied firmly to Farwell School made it the heart and soul of North Charlestown. As long as children remain in those two small classrooms, I'm sure it will remain that way. I truly doubt that Currier and Ives could paint an image that so embodies and reflects life in a traditional rural New Hampshire community.

****

I learned from my childhood experiences that a self-reliant lifestyle is defined and supported by a combination of factors, many of which are embodied in the experiences I have outlined about our life on the farm. Our lives were tied to the rhythms of the changing seasons. We worked hard to survive and took pride in our efforts and the sense of relative independence we gained from it. We learned to respect the land and nature. We utilized the barter system to reduce our dependency on the larger economy and to manage our cost of living. Many times, we simply sacrificed when we could not afford to splurge. We adapted to modern technology where it was affordable and contributed directly to our ability to live as self-sufficiently as we could, and we relied on traditional technologies where it was necessary to make ends meet. We were also part of a larger community that shared our values and lifestyle. Without *all* of these elements working in harmony our lives could hardly be considered self-reliant.

As Scott Hastings often observed in his writings, modern society does not replace or extinguish traditional lifestyles and folkways swiftly, uniformly, or completely. In many places, people cling to the traditional ways of doing things, either out of a sense of nostalgia (because it's part of a shared traditional heritage or craft that has been faithfully passed from generation to generation) or because it makes better sense within the specific limitations of the local economy. When these conditions exist, both modern and traditional lifestyles can co-exist almost side by side and persist that way for many years. This explains very well why that condition existed in my part of the Upper Valley during my childhood and why it also lingers today in the Potomac Highlands of West Virginia.

The truth of the matter is that there were varying degrees of self-reliant lifestyles in the Upper Valley region throughout my childhood. We lived by the core values of self-reliance, but we had technology that prior families living on the same farm did not. On the other side of the coin, we had some people, like Dora Dean, who lived far more traditionally than we did. Our community also had independently wealthy people who had moved in from the outside world and brought with them all the trappings and customs of their outside-world life. They had their own social network, and we simply weren't part of it. We lived separate, but inherently unequal lives.

Change occurred very slowly within that part of the community made up of families who had lived there for generations and worked the land. The rate of change increased when the outsiders moved in with their different ways and replaced the older families. That replacement didn't just occur because the older families sold out and moved away. More often, it occurred when the last generation of an older family passed away and the land was subsequently divided up and sold by children who, like me, had long since left for higher paying jobs and careers elsewhere.

The traditional ways were dying in large part because the generation that practiced, valued, and *relied upon* them was dying, the younger generation was leaving, and a newer, more economically advantaged population from the outside world was moving in to take its place. As this gradual social and economic transformation took root, the alternative value potential of the remaining undeveloped land appreciated accordingly. Over time, the market value of the land became too expensive to sustain and justify the meager economic return that could be obtained from the more traditional pursuits and ways of living. That also made it too expensive for the next generation to afford to live there on the meager, marginal wages that the local economy would support. People earning local wages simply couldn't compete for land with the rising tide of outsiders willing and able to pay much more to live in that setting.

The process of economic transformation begins very gradually and is almost imperceptible to the casual observer. For a time, as long as adequate land resources are available, the two distinct and different societies can occupy the same area, even though they operate in different economic and social dimensions. They can share the community without interfering with one another until the available land resources become too constrained or the basic cost of living begins to change. At that point, the two societies collide and compete with one another for economic supremacy until one or the other is inevitably forced out. Unless politics intervene in the process of what I would call "natural economic selection" or "survival of the wealthiest," the more prosperous economic system will inevitably win the battle.

This is the fundamental cycle of economic transformation that has driven entire Amish communities from one area to another. When land becomes too expensive for people of limited means to purchase in order to sustain a growing family's needs, then the family must move elsewhere to find a place where its lifestyle can be practiced within its proper economic context and constraints. At some point in a money-driven market economy, everything must have the *right* (not necessarily the *highest*) value within its economic context to survive and thrive.

When I was growing up in the Upper Connecticut River Valley, my community appeared to be one of the last remaining economic refuges in New England for self-reliant people. It may exist now only faintly in the northernmost inaccessible reaches of Maine and New Hampshire and in the Northeast Kingdom of Vermont. What traces of it that remained in my community when I left for college appear at the surface to be gone today. Only a period-reminiscent landscape of historic architecture, weather-beaten farm buildings, silent mills, and overgrown farm fields remain. The economic life that built and sustained this landscape has heaved its last breath.

Those who remain from the community I remember and the new people that live there now struggle to maintain and preserve the fleeting relics from that traditional past, but they can't make them vital, useful, or economically relevant again. They are merely polished off, repainted, and put on display. Their economic context and the people who made them useful have quietly and unceremoniously faded away. In essence, many of the older, traditional villages exist today as living ghost towns or museum communities. Even the fresh coats of paint and restored facades cannot resurrect the economic vitality and meaning that the scattered museum pieces once enjoyed. Once the traditional communities and societies pass into history, the most well-intentioned acts of preservation can never truly restore them.

Lifestyle Lost

My adoptive father was generally right about one thing; our lifestyle was an outdated way of living that had no economic future in the modern world. For that reason, my wife and I see ourselves as economic refugees from New England—a people displaced by an economically powerful society that gradually and inevitably smothered the energy out of the simpler traditional society that initially enticed it there. For me, and others like me who lived in and valued that society, all that remains are the memories.

Like the Amish, we have finally moved on to another place where our simple lifestyle values still have some economic, social, and even political relevance. In our case, we chose to retire in Pendleton County, WV. Perhaps now you can understand why our retirement property means so much to us.   While I admit that our modern society has economic advantages that can always, given enough time, supplant a traditional, self-reliant lifestyle, I am left to ponder if it is truly more *sustainable* in the long run. Is it truly able to sustain itself over long periods of time *better* than the alternative lifestyle, even when the market economy isn't so healthy? Is the modern economy a metaphorical hare to the tortoise that represents the more traditional society? That is an interesting question that deserves some additional consideration and contemplation...

North Charlestown Methodist Church (2011)

Farwell School (2011)

Views of Hope Hill Cemetery (2011)

IV. Adjusting to Life in the Outside World

Our childhood upbringing instilled in us a set of firm values and virtues that formed the core philosophical foundation for a self-reliant lifestyle. Chief among them was the virtue of hard work. If you wanted something in life or you wanted to achieve something from your life, you had to work for it. While there is no guarantee that your work will always be rewarded, you can't expect to achieve something in life if you haven't made the effort. The value of something was not measured exclusively in monetary terms; it was also measured by the effort you invested to earn it. Not only was hard work the basis of your own self-esteem and personal integrity, it also earned you the respect of others in the community.

Charity was not to be accepted unreservedly because it would only erode your self-respect and pride. Offers of assistance could be accepted and appreciated as long as an honest effort was made to return the favor when it was *needed,* not only when or if it was *requested.* We recognized that help was occasionally needed and should be offered freely in desperate situations or circumstances, especially when someone was unable to address their own needs. However, that assistance should be provided first and foremost by those who are closest to or benefit most directly or immediately from that person. In this way, the importance of the family, friends, the church, and the community were reinforced.

From these core virtues, other important values were built, such as honesty, honoring your obligations responsibly, treating others fairly and respectfully, and taking responsibility for your actions. If our actions had unintended consequences for others we were obligated to apologize and/or make the situation right. An apology carries little meaning if it isn't followed by corrective action or a change in behavior. Apologizing repeatedly for the same mistake was considered an excuse for the person committing the mistake, not an act of sincere concern for the person who was affected or injured by it.

Another important value to self-reliant people who revere their independence is a deep sense of respect for the sacrifices of those who protect and defend that basic freedom. In our community, that respect was embodied in the only other annual social event, aside from the school

Christmas Pageant—the North Charlestown Memorial Day Commemoration. The central event was a morning parade that began, of course, at Farwell School. From there, the parade marched up the River Road and across the historic Ox Brook stone bridge, where it would pause for a ceremonial gun salute by an Honor Guard. The parade then continued to the Hope Hill Cemetery. Once there, a trumpeter would solemnly play *Taps*, accompanied by a distant echo trumpeter stationed at or near the bridge. The ceremony would be followed by a patriotic public speech to mark the occasion and honor the fallen, whose graves were always colorfully and freshly adorned with flags and fragrant lavender and white lilac bouquets. This commemoration was conducted the same way throughout my childhood and was an important aspect of the community's heritage.

Of course, history has shown that a fine line exists between respectful patriotism and blind, arrogant, and unyielding nationalism. Perhaps the most twisted and immediately recognizable historical example of the gross abuses of nationalism and unbridled patriotic fervor that can arise from blind obedience to authority is the rise of Nazi Germany. Any social institution, including religion, that channels and marshals public thought or beliefs can be illegitimately co-opted and twisted to serve these ends, as evidenced by charismatic leaders such as Hitler, David Koresh, and Jim Jones.

What seems to matter most in determining when this threshold is crossed is the degree to which the patriotic allegiance is manipulated by an individual or a select group of people to strengthen public support for a specific political agenda on the basis of emotion rather than enlightened reason. After carefully reading historical letters and documents, I firmly believe that our forefathers struggled with these issues when debating the appropriate role and structure of our national government. Many of the earliest settlers of our nation understood the implications of political and religious oppression and came to our shores because of it. A self-reliant society cannot function without a meaningful measure of personal liberty and freedom. This cannot be assured when absolute power and authority is vested in an individual or a select group of people who are effectively insulated or removed from the daily lives and struggles of the common citizens that they govern.

Lifestyle Lost

Our parents also taught us another value that would become a source of conflict with our other basic core values and ultimately contribute to the culture shock we experienced in adjusting to the outside world. They routinely instructed us to show respect for people who dressed well and exhibited the marks of financial success, since they were properly rewarded for their education and hard work. While we understood that monetary wealth was not the primary measure of a person's true worth, I can only assume that their true intent was to inspire us to achieve some measure of success in the outside world. If we learned to look up to those people, we might aspire to live like them rather than as we did. However, in the long run, it became a value that we struggled to reconcile with our other core values as we eventually learned how the outside world really worked.

I'm not sure why I have struggled for so many years to make sense of the values I internalized as a child in light of my experiences in the outside world. When I first began to realize that life in the outside world did not always follow or conform to the traditional values and beliefs I had acquired, I honestly felt I could comfortably adjust them to fit my new reality. After all, I had no reason to believe or experience to suggest that the adjustments would be difficult to make. However, I never found it to be easy. It just doesn't seem obvious that it should be so difficult or complicated for intelligent people to do. Nevertheless, in subsequent conversations with other people I have known who have faced similar conflicts with behaviors or beliefs they learned as children, I know I am not alone.

I guess the only way I can understand it is that we must be genetically inclined in some way to adhere fervently to the earliest lessons we learn as children. That seems reasonable to me because humans don't seem to be programmed with all of the instincts we need to survive. As children, we must learn many of the basic skills we will need to function as adults. Given the uncounted thousands of generations that passed before we developed our modern civilization, it is not unreasonable to believe that life in the wilderness would reinforce a strong attachment to our childhood lessons as a fundamental way to ensure our survival. We have only a short time to learn and internalize all the essential skills we would need to survive our independent adulthood, so it is crucial to our survival and success as independent adults that we adhere to them. Perhaps the difficulties we often have in overcoming or adjusting our childhood experiences and values is driven by a residual, instinctive, childhood survival trait that compels us to learn. All I truly understand is that being forced to confront or alter the fundamental values and beliefs we learn as children can be a very difficult and occasionally traumatic adjustment to make.

Over the years, I have coined a term for the crisis of conscience that arises when people are forced to realize that their basic accepted belief system or view of the world is suddenly turned upside down. I call these personal or societal life-changing events "terminal realities." They mark a point in life where one's understanding of the world is abruptly shattered and must be replaced with an entirely new belief system. Once a person's fundamental belief system is shattered in this way, it is impossible to simply ignore it and return to the prior way of thinking. The primary examples I use to explain this concept include a child learning the truth about Santa Claus and the culture shock that the Native Americans experienced after coming into contact with the first European colonists. Both cases represent life-changing turning points that undermine fundamental belief systems, although of quite different magnitude.

When a child learns the truth about Santa Claus, it can create a brief (and often the first) crisis of conscience for the child's implicit trust in his/her parents. It's often shocking to realize that the things you have been taught to believe and accept aren't quite as they seemed. The sudden shock we confront leaves us feeling stunned, helpless, and uncertain of how to react. This paralyzing realization was much more difficult for the Native Americans after first contact with the Europeans. They were faced with the sudden knowledge that the entire world was radically different from their traditional beliefs, and they had to make a difficult choice to adjust them to fit the new reality or abandon the old beliefs and traditions altogether. For the Native Americans, one entire belief system and view of the world came to a sudden and virtually irretrievable end and had to be replaced with a radically different one.

The attack on Pearl Harbor, the assassination of President Kennedy, and the terrorist attacks of 9/11 caused many Americans to rethink elements of our own belief systems and personal liberties, although to a far lesser degree than first contact with Europeans did to the Native Americans. In all three instances, we were forced to consider sacrificing some of our basic societal expectations regarding personal freedom in exchange for a greater sense of personal security. Even these relatively subtle changes were significant enough to ingrain these events in our national conscience so deeply that people who experienced them can still remember clearly where they were and what they were doing when they occurred. Terminal realities are not to be taken lightly, regardless of how earth-shattering they may be.

The Amish actually utilize the concept of terminal reality to foster a greater appreciation of their culture and heritage in their children and to help them make a deliberate choice to adopt them. In a traditional rite of passage into adulthood known as "rumspringa," Amish parents send their children away to immerse themselves in the culture of the modern outside world for an extended period of time. They are strongly encouraged to experience the culture shock of a sudden and dramatic exposure to a vastly different value system and standard of behavior. In doing so, it gives their children an opportunity to sow their wild oats through the experience. In most instances, they return to the community with a greater understanding and appreciation for their traditional values and different culture that strengthens their determination to preserve them and live by them. For those who choose to live in the outside world, the experience results in a life-changing terminal reality.

I believe that the culture shock that I experienced when I moved away from the farm was similar to the Amish rite of rumspringa, except for us, it was understood that there was no going back. Our childhood experiences were not as different from the outside world as they are for Amish children, but our basic value system proved to be very different. Perhaps those values were not as different in words as they were in application or practice. Whatever the case may be, as I gradually learned how the outside world really worked, I discovered many conflicts with the core values I had internalized that tarnished the initial image I had of the larger, modern society. Like an Amish teenager, I struggled to decide if I needed to fundamentally adjust my childhood core values to relieve the moral conflicts or hold firmly onto them and just disregard the inconsistent values and virtues of the outside world. Since I went into the modern world with great hope and anticipation, it was not an easy decision to make. Unbeknownst to me at the time, I would ultimately struggle with it for more than 25 years.

Lifestyle Lost

****

Our traditional farming life began to end before I left for college. I had started assuming regular farm chores when I was six. This work continued with gradual changes in my responsibilities as I grew older, until 1977, when I turned fifteen. Around that time, my father's health began to deteriorate as he developed advanced emphysema and farmer's lung, and he could no longer keep up with the demands of farm work. By 1978, we began selling the land and eventually the cows and equipment to pay the growing cost of treatment. Small farm operators usually can't afford the luxury of expensive medical insurance, dental plans, and retirement plans. The value of the land is all they have. Before long, the fate of our past was sealed, and there was no choice but to move away to find a new life. We had to learn a new way to survive in a world that we didn't fully understand.

Consequently in 1977, I accepted my first paid job off the farm. I became the janitor of Farwell School. On the way home from high school, I would get off the school bus at Farwell School, do my cleaning work, then walk home to finish my homework, load the woodbox with firewood or do whatever routine chores remained. School homework had to be done later in the evening or on weekends. My janitorial duties included sweeping the floors, cleaning the windows, cleaning the bathrooms, mopping the basement floors, emptying the trash, and chasing out the bats that occasionally roosted in the dark recesses of the school's basement. Later in the year, I was asked to design a layout for the small basement library that was completed in the following year. I guess you can say that was my first planning design experience.

I kept that job for a year and passed it along to my sisters and mother. I then worked a series of other brief entry-level, menial jobs over the next ten years that provided a little extra spending money and helped carry me through college. My work experiences over that period were wide and varied, with most of them occurring after I started college. In addition to janitorial work, I had worked briefly as an inventory-taker for Retail Grocers Inventory Service (RGIS), a news stringer (reporter) covering Claremont City Council meetings for WECM radio, a short order cook, a surveyor's assistant, a house painter, a carpenter's/electrician's assistant,

76

a shipper/receiver at a computer company warehouse, an assembly line worker and quality control inspector at a different plant, and a research assistant for a college professor in graduate school. Eventually, I was able to land two city planning internships along the way, one in Hartford, Connecticut and another in Portland, Maine.

Prior to moving away to college, my experiences were largely limited to the farm. We had little interaction with people in the business world and virtually no understanding of what outside life was like. Even getting a job was an intimidating experience because we had no real work experience, and we didn't always know what skills were needed or expected for outside jobs. All of us were somewhat intimidated by the outside business world, and I freely admit that this fear was a stronger influence in my decision to go to college than any interest in pursuing a specific future career. I had no firm idea of what work I really wanted to do or would be best suited to do. All I knew was that going on to college would give me time to figure out what I should do with my life and exposure to people who had a better understanding of and connections with the outside world. I had no better idea of how to understand and adjust to life in the modern world.

After years of being told there was no future in farming or the way we lived, we were all quite motivated to enter the modern society, despite our concerns and fears. We had far too little appreciation for the traditional folkways that framed our childhood experiences. They were considered relics from an outmoded way of living that had no place or meaning in the outside world. It may have been correct to see them as relics, but it was not correct to assume that they had no value in modern society. We simply didn't understand that distinction.

Many of the new people I met in college found my childhood experiences unbelievable or humorous. I also had a strong rural New Hampshire accent that made me sound out of place—even in Connecticut. I became very conscious of how I talked and worked hard to alter my patterns of speech. I certainly didn't want to be forever perceived as an outsider in the society into which I was moving. I had never even used an escalator before I went to college, and my first awkward attempt was a source of chiding from my college friends. There were no escalators in the Claremont/Springfield area when I grew up, and I don't believe there has been a need to build any since.

I seemed so obviously out of place that one student from a wealthy family in New Jersey actually asked me if I needed a visa to go to school in Connecticut. Adapting to my new life would require many years of work and major changes in my natural behavior patterns.

To avoid feeling different or odd, I quickly learned to put the memories, patterns, and behaviors of my childhood lifestyle behind me. I certainly wasn't proud of my past and my farming heritage as I now realize I should have been. In fact, I learned to be ashamed of it by a rapidly changing society that viewed such traditional lifestyles at best as outdated and at worst as regressive or an impediment to progress. I was exposed to many useful life skills during my childhood that would eventually help me live a more self-reliant lifestyle, but at that point in my life, they had no use or apparent value in the outside world. I find I have to relearn many of them today either because I never paid close attention to them when I was younger, or the memories have faded from a lack of appreciation or meaningful use.

In December 1986, I completed six years of college and left the University of California at Berkeley with a Master's Degree in City Planning. I had already earned a Bachelor's Degree in Sociology and a Certificate in Applied Social Research from the University of Hartford, Connecticut. Those are impressive-sounding titles to effectively confirm that I spent a lot of money I didn't have to obtain a few fancy pieces of paper. By the time I had graduated, I had accumulated so much student loan debt (through three separate loans) that I had to pay between $30,000 and $40,000 (including interest) to retire it all. Still, I managed to pay it all off in slightly less than the required ten years. Perhaps I managed to learn the virtue of frugality from my self-reliant upbringing, after all. My wife will attest that I have always been very conservative when it comes to our finances.

I read an article in the October 2, 2011 edition of the Cumberland, MD Times-News expressing great concern over the level of student loan debt that students must now assume just to get a college education.[iii] According to the communications manager of the Consumer Credit Counseling Service of Maryland and Delaware, the average student loan debt at graduation is about $23,000. I'm sorry to say that I had to chuckle at that because I grew up in rural poverty and left college nearly 25 years earlier with considerably more debt than that (not adjusted for inflation). Even with that level of debt, my parents still had to contribute a lot of money that my father's mother had left behind for our education when she died. So, you might ask, why didn't I obtain scholarships or a federal grant to help with the expenses? The answer to that question was the first disappointing lesson I learned about how the outside world works.

First of all, let me say that I did get a scholarship that was renewed for all four of my undergraduate years and an out-of-state tuition waiver for a portion of my graduate work at the University of California. I also worked a number of different summer jobs every year and three others while I was attending school. At the urging of my high school guidance counselor, I also applied for a Pell Grant, which is a federal program that is designed to help needy students with college expenses. Now I won't claim that I graduated from high school with grades that made me appear to be a junior Albert Einstein, but my grades weren't the primary factor in my eligibility for the grant. I met the basic requirements, so the program's final decision had nothing to do with my grades.

I was rejected for the Pell Grant because my parents owned property that made them appear (on paper) to be far wealthier than we were. It didn't matter that they needed that land to survive or that my father needed to sell it to pay his medical expenses. As far as the administrative entity was concerned, my parents had plenty of land they could sell to put their five kids through school. That was the reason we were given for my denial. We were proud people, so we never let rejection make us bitter. It was something we were used to, so we accepted it without an argument. We never wanted to feel entitled to charity.

Sometime around the middle of my tenure at the University of Hartford, I became well acquainted with a student who happened to be a refugee from South Vietnam. Over the course of our association, I quickly acquired a deep respect for him and his determination to adjust to life in America. I never let his story bother me, because he never knew how I was treated by the Pell Grant program, but his experience with the program was a greater disappointment to me with respect to the program's integrity than my own rejection.

Lifestyle Lost

One day, shortly after the semester began, he returned to his dorm room bearing a check that he was quite pleased with. He was always a cheerful man, but his satisfaction was bubbling over, and I just had to ask what he was so happy about. Now, I must explain that his family was *not* poor. I never knew or cared how wealthy they were, and it really doesn't matter. He had previously told me how his family was among the last to be airlifted from the U.S. Consulate in Saigon when South Vietnam fell at the end of the war. In describing their escape, he told me that his parents instructed him and each of his brothers and sisters to wear as much gold and silver as they could carry during their harrowing evacuation. However, as a refugee, he was awarded a Pell Grant that paid the full cost of his tuition expenses.

He told me that the check he had received was the grant payment for that semester. It had been sent directly to the university more than a month earlier. After the university received the grant payment, his father sent the college a personal check for the full tuition payment—even though the bill had been paid by the grant. Once his father's payment was received, he went to the Bursar's Office to collect a check for the overpayment, which was the check he had received. He was placing that check, along with all of the past overpayment checks he had collected over his years at the university, into a special savings account that he eventually used as a down payment to buy his first home after he graduated. I never asked and he never said what benefit his father received from this odd transaction, but I assumed that it was financially advantageous for his father to overpay the tuition bill rather than giving the money to his son directly.

In essence, the Pell Grant program provided a huge down payment for his first house. My reward for growing up in poverty on a farm was the responsibility to pay more than $30,000 in student loan debt while also paying income taxes for all the money I earned over the entire ten-year repayment schedule. This is not the standard of integrity I had learned growing up in the society of self-reliance. Perhaps this story further explains why I had to chuckle after reading a story about how the high cost of college education and student debt is hurting our students. I agree that it is, but I have to wonder if people truly understand the broader reasons why problems like this exist. From my perspective, critical thinking has truly become a lost art.

****

I thoroughly enjoyed my years in college. I met a lot of different people from diverse backgrounds and experiences that I never would have met on the farm. I gained a better understanding of how the outside world worked that eased my transition into a new and quite different life. The biggest challenge I faced after graduation was getting my first job in my chosen profession, which I assumed would be the final hurdle in my transition to a modern way of living.

Although I had lived in the shadows of two major cities during my college years, I still preferred to live in rural settings. The excitement and entertainment opportunities afforded by life in the city were strong attractions to young, single people like me, but I had great difficulties adjusting to many aspects of city life. The noise and confusion from all the hustle and bustle always contributed to the stress I felt living in such a hectic environment. I was never able to just filter it out like other people seemed to do instinctively. I would often complain about some noise that was bothering me while others around me would say they hadn't noticed it. Little noises would always wake me up at night. My roommates would say that I was just a light sleeper, but I always had a sense that I wasn't adjusting well to all the late-night activity.

The formality of urban life was another problem for me. Everyone dressed either stylishly or formally. I was never comfortable dressing up in a suit or in trendy clothes. It didn't feel natural to me, and I certainly didn't look natural dressed that way. I didn't even learn how to tie a necktie until I was in college. Even then, I kept a couple of ties loosely tied after I took them off just so I wouldn't have to figure out how to retie them the next time I needed to wear them.

I was always afraid that I looked as out of place to everyone else as I did to myself when I looked in a mirror. I was sure that other people wouldn't believe that my personality or character really belonged in a suit or even fashionable leisurewear. When I had finally advanced far enough in my career that I was expected to wear a suit daily, I refused to keep it on after I left work. By the time I got through the door from work or a night meeting, I would already be carrying my suit jacket, and I'd be loosening my tie to take it off. Within the first ten minutes after I was in the house, I would be back in my casual clothes—none of which would classify as stylish by any objective standards. Just ask my wife.

To ease my transition into the professional world, I decided to apply for jobs at regional planning commissions in rural New England. It seemed reasonable that I could focus more on learning the ropes of my new career if I wasn't saddled with concerns about the annoying anxieties of city life. I applied for any and all regional planning jobs I could find in Vermont, New Hampshire, and Maine. However, there were few entry-level job openings, and the competition was quite tough at that time. The northern New England economy wasn't very healthy (we were just heading into the 1987 stock market crash and recession), and many of the applicants I was competing with for entry-level jobs had some prior experience in planning. My Master's degree from the University of California would usually get me an interview, but not the job.

I decided that I needed some practical experience to improve my chances, but how was I to get it if I couldn't get the job without it? This is the classic chicken-or-the-egg conundrum that all recent college graduates face whenever the job market is tight. After a couple of months of searching, I realized I needed to get my first job soon or I would be facing a series of huge monthly college debt payments with no income to pay them, much less cover my living expenses. I was stuck at my mother's new home in the Lakes Region of New Hampshire (where she had moved in late 1986 after selling the farm) without a job prospect.

My solution to the problem was to make an appointment to speak with the executive director of the local regional planning commission, which was centered in Meredith, NH. I told him that I had been interviewing for planning jobs and that I had a strong interest in regional planning. I explained the problems I was having competing with more experienced planners for entry-level jobs. I also told him about the college debt that I was facing, and that I desperately needed to find a job in planning, or I'd have to consider some other line of work to pay for it. Since I didn't have anything else to do with my time right then, I asked him if he had some planning work that I could volunteer to do between my job interviews. I wasn't asking to be paid, because I felt that the work experience would be valuable to me in my job search. All I asked from him was a reference if he felt my work was good. I had no problem with this arrangement, because I was confident I could prove myself if I could just get an opportunity to demonstrate what I could do.

Apparently, this was not an offer that planning administrators or supervisors typically receive, even though it made good and simple sense to me. As I waited for his response, I could sense his amazement and bewilderment about how to react or what to say. He certainly appreciated my offer, but he felt it wouldn't be appropriate for me to work without pay. Perhaps he could empathize with my situation. Whatever his motivations were, he offered me a paid internship to help write a grant for one of the towns in his region. At that point, it was my turn to be shocked. This was a great opportunity because I would be getting work experience *and* earning money. Maybe it wasn't a living wage, but I could stay at my mother's house until I could find a full-time salaried position. That's how I landed my first planning job without even responding to a job ad.

Although I had been to college, I still didn't know anything about how to work in a professional office environment. All of my work experience at that time had been on a farm or in a traditional blue-collar work setting. I was finally joining the ranks of the professional work force, so I approached it the way I thought a professional should—whatever that was. I went out and bought virtually all of the office supplies I thought I would need. I bought a briefcase, stapler, tape dispenser, a desktop calendar stand, a desk blotter, and a bunch of other items that the agency kept in something called an "office supply closet." How was I to know about that? It wasn't something I had learned in school. You can imagine how surprised I was to appear for my first day of work and learn I didn't need to buy all those things on my own. However, I can report to you that today, nearly 25 years after I started that job, I still have and use some of those supplies I bought in 1987. I actually expect to take them with me into retirement.

Fortunately, my basic theory worked. Within three months after I began working as a paid intern at the Lakes Region Planning Commission, I got my first offer of salaried employment at the Central Massachusetts Regional Planning Commission in Worcester. It wasn't a permanent position, but it was a start, and it offered me the money I needed to begin making payments on my student loans. As it turned out, it was a grant-funded position that would last only as long as the grant funding continued. I would ultimately be responsible for a portion of the work funded by the grant, and I would be responsible for writing additional grants to extend the funding. It didn't sound to me like a job with a stable future, but it was an opportunity to begin pursuing the career I had sought. For the time being, I decided that it was the best opportunity I would receive. With my college loan deferment period rapidly closing, I wasn't willing to risk a job offer to continue searching for a more permanent one.

Again, I had to face the prospect of living in a city environment, albeit a relatively small one. I still found myself retreating to rural New Hampshire on most weekends, if for no other reason than to get a good night's sleep. I lived in an apartment building just outside downtown Worcester that was a couple of buildings away from one of the city's two major hospitals. I found the sound of the ambulance sirens coming and going at all times of the night much harder to sleep through than the night calls of the loons on Lake Winnipesaukee near my mother's new house. Traveling back to New Hampshire on the weekends also allowed me to maintain contact with my former co-workers at the Lakes Region Planning Commission and gave me an opportunity to do odd jobs in my spare time for the agency.

It was good to know that my former boss at the Lakes Region Planning Commission liked my work and wanted me to return. During my absence, he managed to drum up enough contract work to offer me a permanent paid position nearly four months after I had accepted the job in Worcester. I gratefully accepted and left the Central Massachusetts Regional Planning Commission after successfully completing the application for the next round of grant funding. I felt that my professional career was finally gaining legitimacy and that I had cleared the last remaining hurdle on my way to a new and promising life in the outside world. At that time, roughly seven years had passed since I left the farm to attend college. Nevertheless, I had a lot more to learn about life in modern society than I ever realized or wanted to believe.

Lifestyle Lost

****

My enthusiasm for the field of planning was unbounded in my early years. I wanted to do and learn anything and everything. Regional planning, in particular, was a really great position from which to learn the practical realities of the planning field while working in a rural environment. The job allowed me to work with a number of different cities and towns and to learn practical applications in a wide range of planning issues, from housing to transportation to land use to economic development. Regional planning helps small towns and cities serve their own planning needs without having to hire their own staffs or expensive consultants. It also helps communities address critical common or shared needs and issues that they could not otherwise address by themselves. Consequently, the job provided both a wide range of experiences and opportunities to work with many different communities. This was just the type of work I needed to understand how the professional world functioned.

One important and memorable lesson came early. At some point in my first year at the Lakes Region Planning Commission, a major political scandal erupted in Laconia (the largest community in the region) that involved the mayor and the city's own planning director. Apparently, the mayor had been caught taking kickbacks or extorting funds from the developer of a major residential development called Sundown Shores in exchange for required project approvals and permits. A team of FBI agents raided the city's planning office and carried away more than 30 boxes of evidence to support their case. The planning director was eventually fired and the mayor was arrested. With the city's planning department left in complete disarray, our agency was called upon to provide planning support until the issue was resolved and a new planning director could be hired.

Our agency's senior planner, a good and long-time professional friend and colleague of mine, became the city's temporary lead planner to oversee the department's functions during the transition. All of us chipped in under his direction to help keep their various projects moving forward over the recovery period. I had only limited knowledge of what had occurred in the city's planning department, but the lesson I gained from it about the political hazards that can arise in local government planning stayed with me for many years.

Lifestyle Lost

I had learned planning as a technical field that required a certain professional expertise. However, the Laconia scandal taught me that the world of politics has long arms and tendrils that extend far beyond the offices of the elected officials. I came to realize that planners had to exercise a great deal of political savvy to negotiate the potential minefield of local politics that can trap and swallow you whole, as it did the city's planning director. Suddenly, the job didn't seem as easy as it did learning about it from textbooks and class lectures. It forced me to hold tightly to my conscience and my values, as I moved forward cautiously through my planning career.

I worked for four years in New Hampshire and Vermont as a regional planner before being offered my first supervisory position. I had met and married my wife (Barbara) while working briefly at a regional planning office in Middlebury, Vermont, when I was offered a promotion to senior planner at another regional planning office in Macon, Georgia. This move was a big leap for us in a number of ways.

I had never even traveled more than a few miles south of the Ohio River when I accepted the Macon job. At the time, we were living in a mobile home in a trailer park next to an aircraft manufacturing plant in nearby Vergennes, VT, and we couldn't afford to buy a home on our combined salaries. The price of land in Vermont had become so expensive that it was virtually impossible to afford the mortgage cost on local wages. The large debt payments I had to pay (for both my education and car) didn't make it any easier. However, housing was much more affordable in Macon, Georgia, and we were able to buy our first house there. Nearly six months after we moved into the house, our only son, Michael was born. People say that the most stressful, life-changing events that we experience are getting married, having our first child, and buying our first home. We did all three in the span of seven months in 1991. In the process, we became economic refugees from New England.

Regional planning agencies in the deep south are much larger and more diverse operations than the agencies I had worked for in New England. The New England agencies offered simple planning and mapping services, with a little grant-writing assistance to support their specific planning initiatives. The bigger southern agencies offered broader planning and mapping services, grant-writing and economic development services, rural public transit administration, and a variety of aging or elderly service programs.

My work in Macon was quite rewarding in several ways. As the agency's new senior planner, I was hired to supervise a planning department with a full-time professional staff of six. Within my first year, I was promoted to planning director, with a commensurate salary raise. A couple of years later, I was elected to the board of directors of the Georgia Planner's Association, a state chapter of the American Planning Association, as a central region representative. I saw this as a real opportunity to influence the professional planning agenda, but it turned out to be another lesson in the realities of professional politics.

During the early 1990s, communities across the country were struggling to comply with the EPA's new RCRA Subtitle D regulations that required old municipal dumps to be replaced with lined sanitary landfills. The purpose of this change was to prevent contamination of groundwater resources from leachate that gradually seeps from household waste buried in unlined landfills or dumps. The principle of the requirement was sound, but the expense of the transition caused the cost of waste disposal to rise significantly. Planners across the nation were scrambling to find ways to effectively manage these costs, and reducing unnecessary sources of household waste was a logical top priority. At that time, one of the biggest sources of unnecessary waste was unsolicited or junk mail. Since the public hated being inundated with junk mail, it was not only an effective way to reduce both the volume and disposal cost of household waste, it was also very popular with voters.

As a professional planner working to convince citizens and businesses of the need to reduce the volume of waste generated by junk mail, I was dismayed by the volume of unsolicited mail I routinely received from the American Planning Association (APA). Throughout my planning career, I received scores of promotional solicitations from the APA to join various programs and to purchase books and special services they offered. To me, it made no sense for our own professional organization to practice a marketing activity that its own members were fighting to control.

Lifestyle Lost

As a member of the Georgia Planning Association's board of directors, I managed to get our association to send a letter to the APA's board of directors formally requesting that they end the practice of sending unsolicited mail to its professional membership. We felt that we had a good chance of being heard, because the newly elected president of the national association was from our neighboring state of Alabama. However, the response we eventually received from the APA was a rejection of our request. While the APA considered and appreciated our suggestion, they ultimately decided that it was not in the organization's best interest to comply because their mail solicitation efforts were too effective.

In the end, our own professional organization decided that it was in its own financial best interest to continue a practice that its dues-paying members were actively preaching against to save money for our local governments and their taxpayers. Is it any wonder why we were fighting a losing battle with the business community on this issue? As a professional planner, I was paying over $100 in annual dues to the APA to represent our interests. This attitude was a deep blow to my respect for the organization. I eventually resigned from the board and never again ran for elected office in the APA or any of its chapters.

Also, during my first two years in Macon, I witnessed a significant incident within the regional planning community, when the grant-writing functions of several regional planning commissions came under increased scrutiny from the Georgia Department of Community Affairs. The first agency audited for program irregularities was one of our neighboring regions in Milledgeville. The state eventually determined that certain essential documents were missing or never completed, and the agency could not clearly document how federal grant funds were spent. The agency was forced to close its doors, and the counties it served were divided into the neighboring regions. Our agency received four of them as new members, before it was all said and done.

The state's auditing probe then moved on to other regional agencies that had been previously questioned about poor or inconsistent grant documentation patterns. Our agency was one of the commissions that were targeted. It was a very tense episode for our entire staff. I remember the director of our grant-writing department knocking on my door several times wanting to talk with me about her fears over the impending audit. She desperately reviewed dozens of boxes of old grant files trying to make sure that all of the documentation was still intact. Agencies of that size produce reams of documents that have to be stored over long periods of time. Regardless of whether or not any improper actions are deliberately taken, it is not difficult for critical documents to be misplaced, separated, or accidentally discarded by another department or program seeking storage space for its own critical documents. Filing and storage space was always at a premium, and everyone was competing for space to keep their own administrative files.

The specter of a major state audit also triggered panic throughout the other programs. I tended to be less concerned about it, since I had been hired only recently and couldn't be held personally responsible for any actions by my predecessors. My biggest concern was the possibility that our entire agency might be shut down if any serious problems were uncovered during the audit. Those who had worked at the office for years were also understandably concerned that their professional reputations might be forever tarnished by any lingering allegations of impropriety. This fear among the staff eventually built into rumors and back-stabbing as long-time colleagues sought ways to distance or insulate themselves from those most closely associated with the state's concerns.

As the date for the audit approached, new concerns emerged as the Macon Telegraph sought to understand and cover the story. The agency's executive director was drawn into question for his outside personal business activities. He operated his own home-based flower and wedding planning business. Questions were raised regarding whether or not his personal business was being conducted during regular office hours. Eventually, everyone in the office was worried about the next revelation in the spiraling swirl of allegations.

Once the state's audit was completed, our agency was completely cleared of any alleged problems. The allegations surrounding the executive director's outside business activities became a brief butt of jokes, but they, too, soon passed. The episode persuaded me to start my own private consulting firm with some friends from the former regional agency in Milledgeville. We called our firm Innovative Planning Concepts, and we managed to secure a few small contracts from communities outside my agency's region. My executive director never liked my decision to do outside work, but it was not illegal for me to work for communities outside our region as long as it didn't conflict with my primary job. I decided I needed to do it for two reasons—to preserve my growing reputation as a planner should the agency have been shut down and to make sure I had some source of income to help me survive any potential transition period.

The agency survived the audit, but the relationships between the staff were never the same. After months of rumors and innuendoes between long-time colleagues, little trust remained. The executive director in particular felt slighted by staff and didn't know who he could really trust. What had been a good and supportive office environment when I arrived gradually eroded and many people began to leave. I worked there for another year-and-a-half before the toll of overall work demands, both inside and outside the office, became too much to bear. I eventually moved on to other jobs and left the consulting firm I had started in Macon.

The job in Macon was a real turning point for my planning career. Over my three-and-a-half-year tenure, I was promoted to planning director, elected to serve on the state's planning association, and had started my own private consulting firm. I had also survived the agency's turmoil unscathed by all of the wild allegations. In the process, I learned quite well about the stress that working in and around the world of politics can exact.

In talking with my friends, I would explain how life in planning was completely different from life on the farm. Both require hard work. After a full day of work on the farm you would be exhausted, but you knew you had accomplished something, and you slept well through the night. After a full day of planning work, I was mentally exhausted, but found it increasingly difficult to sleep through the night. I would wake up worried that I wouldn't be able to meet my deadlines or that I had forgotten to do something. I would have to make notes or write out a detailed work schedule just to get it off my mind before I could get back to sleep.

I was also bothered by the actions I saw local officials taking that I felt was wrong. At that time, I didn't feel I had the authority or influence to prevent or stop them without jeopardizing my career. None of them were as serious as what I had seen occur in Laconia, but they still violated the core principles I was taught. While I never let myself fall into that trap, the knowledge that I had not called attention to them bothered me and conflicted with my conscience. I found myself losing sleep more and more frequently as I learned the inconvenient truth about how government really works. I just felt as though I was powerless to change it despite how uncomfortable it became to live with my knowledge of it.

I learned another influential lesson from my wife's work while we were living in Macon that would affect my impressions and understanding of the outside world. In early 1992, roughly four months after Michael was born, Barb landed a job as an audit clerk at the Chapter 13 Trustee's office in Macon. She had worked in banking previously, and her financial experience was helpful in reviewing bankruptcy filings. While working as a loan agent and mortgage originator for small banks, she had an opportunity to help people learn to manage their finances responsibly and achieve their ambitions, whether it was buying their first home or a new car. She had a view that the banking industry could help people move ahead and improve their lives. This was the sense of personal satisfaction she took from the job. It was her work as a Chapter 13 audit clerk that opened her eyes to the dark side of personal financing and introduced us to the larger institutional problems that would eventually undermine our economy and help bring about the "Great Recession" of the early twenty-first century.

After auditing scores of bankruptcy filings, Barb began to notice some troubling patterns that, at that time, were relatively new and largely unknown trends. Many of the filings she reviewed revealed a consistent pattern of people who had received more credit cards and lines of credit than they could ever afford to pay off. With little knowledge of what they were really doing, they used their credit cards so frivolously and irresponsibly that the minimum monthly payments could not cover the interest that was accruing on their principal balances. As the principle grew monthly from their reckless spending patterns and spiraling interest debt, they eventually reached a point where they could no longer even afford the minimum payments and filed for bankruptcy.

Lifestyle Lost

This situation is well understood today, but it came as a complete surprise to us at that time. Without exception throughout our married life, my wife and I have *never* paid any interest on the expenses we have charged to our credit cards. We have always paid the full amount of our outstanding credit card balance each month. If we couldn't afford to pay for the items we purchased with our credit cards, we wouldn't purchase them. We essentially used our credit cards as short-term, interest-free loans, until the monthly cycle closed and we received our bill. The thought that someone would treat their *credit line* as a form of unlimited cash to which they were *entitled* was completely alien to us. Our experience was based on the lessons I learned from a self-reliant upbringing: don't buy what you can't afford.

The patterns we saw from Barb's experience made it easier for us to understand why some of our neighbors and friends—who we knew could not be earning the incomes we earned—were able to live such comparatively lavish lifestyles. It appeared to us that America had found a new way to generate wealth that the economy wasn't creating quickly enough through growth in the supply of money. We had moved into the era of creative credit. If people didn't have in hand the money they needed to live the lifestyle that they desired, they could borrow on their futures. This strategy eventually fueled the economic booms of the 1990s and early twenty-first century.

Soon, it became apparent to me that middle class Americans *owned* significantly less of the lifestyles they possessed than previous generations. When they reached the end of their ability to afford the minimum monthly payments for their borrowed lives, they could simply file for bankruptcy and, for only a portion of the true cost, reset their finances. There was so much unbridled greed for economic profit from these creative financing schemes, that credit was soon extended again to people who recently emerged from bankruptcy. The schemes were also extended to other forms of lending, from car purchases to home mortgages.

This was the pattern of exaggerated credit and inflated value within the broader economy that inevitably led to the mortgage lending meltdown of 2007. We are now realizing the price we must pay for all of the bad debt that was deferred from decades of unsecured wealth and consumption. Eventually, all the hedge funds (which had a similar effect on credit markets as the derivatives that precipitated the 1987 Stock Market Crash) packaged from inherently worthless high-risk loans could not be supported or backed by actual resources available within the economy. A serious economic adjustment was inevitable, and we could see it coming in the early 1990s. It was only a matter of when.

At the time, we felt that our best defense against the impending collapse was to avoid excessive debt. Barb went on to future jobs at banks and credit unions and paid closer attention to debt-to-income ratios. We continued to rely on the fiscally conservative values that self-reliant living teaches. It was the best approach to the problem that we felt we could take.

****

After a brief experience as the first planning director of LaGrange, Georgia, I moved on to my final regional planning job as planning director for the East Alabama Regional Planning and Development Commission (EARPDC) in Anniston. It was during this job that I reached the pinnacle of my planning career. I inherited a staff of six full-time planners and cartographers that grew to a record of twelve during my tenure, which lasted over 7.5 years. My department's overall annual budget increased from roughly $600,000 per year when I started to more than $2 million before I left. In 2004, my final year at the agency, I received the first Distinguished Leadership in Planning award from the Alabama Chapter of the American Planning Association. I enjoyed my years at the EARPDC and my working relationship with my colleagues at the agency and all of the other people with whom we associated in the regional planning community. They were among the best and most personally rewarding years I have had in my regional planning career.

Of course, a major reason for my personal satisfaction was derived from the fact that we had returned to an environment with which I was quite familiar—the Appalachian Mountains. While living in the rolling plains of central Georgia, we made many excursions into the North Georgia mountains, just to remind us of home in northern New England. We even searched for a small plot of land that we could buy and pay off over time, so that we could eventually sell our home in Macon and build a retirement home on it. However, the land in that area was already overpriced by demand from the metro Atlanta area, and we never did find the property we were seeking. Without realizing it at the time, our futile search set the pattern that would eventually result in the purchase of our current retirement property in Pendleton County, WV.

Most people don't realize that Alabama has mountains even though, in all honesty, they aren't very big. We lived in the Anniston/Oxford area, which was within 25 miles of the state's highest point, Cheaha Mountain. Its maximum elevation is 2,405 feet above sea level, but the views of it from Anniston and from its lofty summit are truly beautiful. The Anniston area is at the center of all the state's highest summits, with a total of five peaks over 2,000 feet. We relished our return to the mountains and made many camping and hiking trips throughout the highlands region of northeast Alabama. My attachment to the landscape also made it easier for me to feel attached to the small mountain communities I served that were nestled within the shallow valleys, gaps, and hollows. We never regretted a minute of the nearly eight years we spent living in the Anniston area.

It was during my tenure at the agency in Alabama that I searched for and found my biological family. In July 1998, I managed to locate and establish contact with them. I discovered that I had a total of seven biological brothers and sisters. I had two full sisters and one full brother, as well as one half-sister and three half-brothers. My biological mother and father were married in October 1962, about eight months after I was born and less than six months after I had been placed for adoption. The fact that they retrieved my older full sister from a foster home placement that occurred at the same time I was placed for adoption convinced me that they had tried to block my adoption. That intervention effort also helped explain the irregularities that we found in my adoption records and process.

It was initially interesting to learn that I had many similarities and differences with my biological family. Both families lived on the edge of poverty throughout my childhood years, but they lived quite different lifestyles. While I grew up on a farm in rural New Hampshire, my biological siblings were raised in relatively urban settings in the New Hampshire seacoast region. Most of their lives were spent moving between small cities, including Portsmouth (where my younger brother and I were born), Rochester, and Haverhill, Massachusetts (where my biological mother was born).

Two of my half-brothers did gain some practical experience in self-reliant living. At the age of sixteen, they left home and hitch-hiked their way across the country. As they moved from community to community, they would get temporary jobs to earn a little spending money to carry them through the next stage in their journeys. They even happened to meet by accident one time while traveling separately in opposite directions. These two brothers and their older sister managed to live far more independent lives than two of my full siblings. They never felt as though they were part of my father's family, because they were my mother's children from her late previous husband.

By and large, especially in their younger years, my biological brothers and sisters had childhood experiences that taught them to be street-wise and to understand how to work the system to their advantage as urban survival strategies. I, on the other hand, learned how to live a self-reliant lifestyle as a survival strategy against rural poverty. Both were practical, common-sense approaches to the challenges created by our different environments, but they arose from and instilled very different core values.

As I grew to know my biological family over the years, the differences in our values and approach to living became apparent. Several of my biological siblings had extensive experiences with drugs and alcohol. In my adoptive family, only my adopted sister became involved with drugs and alcohol and only *after* she left the family and moved to a larger city. None of us were at all involved with them during our childhoods.

A number of my biological siblings also learned how to take advantage of loopholes in various public assistance programs as well as creative ways to make or acquire money when necessary. Many of them had filed bankruptcies—some more than once. I only began to understand after leaving the farm that people in the outside world eventually learn how to manipulate the system to their advantage, like my Vietnamese friend in college. The mere thought of looking for and taking advantage of loopholes in the system clashed with my basic value system. It wasn't something that would occur to me, because I was focused on earning what I needed in life, not looking for a way to outwit the system.

As I gained experience in the planning field, I soon realized that many people actively seek to find loopholes in the rules to avoid what they see as undue expense or economic injustice. It is an attitude that I find prevalent in many aspects of our society, from zoning regulations to taxes. It is one of the practical experiences in my career that has trained me, and most other professional planners, to think about the potential loopholes when writing regulations. It is the only way to defend the integrity of the rules we write and ensure that the public interests we are trying to protect are not compromised by the way people abuse them.

To me, it's one of the sad commentaries on the overall integrity of our basic values. In writing about it, I am reminded of a scene from the 1997 movie, <u>Contact</u>. In it, the lead character (Ellie Arroway) is approached by her former boss (David Drumlin) who was chosen as an astronaut over her by misrepresenting his true values and misleading the selection committee into believing that he was their perfect choice. Ellie lost the competition because she tried to answer the committee's questions as honestly as she could, despite the fact that she felt they were unfair. Privately, Drumlin apologized for his actions and told her how he wished the world was the kind of place where the integrity she had demonstrated before the committee was rewarded. Her simple response to him was, "I thought the world was what we make of it." I think that statement best reflects my own sentiments about the declining integrity I have witnessed in our nation's basic value system.

****

When I finally met my biological father for the first time in late 1998, I realized that I would have very little time to get to know him. He was 75 years old at that time and in declining health. He suffered from both Alzheimer's and Parkinson's, and his mobility was limited by the multiple strokes and heart attacks that he had suffered over the years. I did my best to spend time with him, including an effort I made in 1999 to relocate back to New Hampshire. But, as we learned, it was not easy to sell our home in Oxford, Alabama after a nearby large military installation closed and took the bottom out of the local housing market. Eventually, in June 2004, I was offered a job in Charles County, Maryland (halfway between our home in Alabama and my parent's newest home in New Hampshire). After accepting the job, I called my mother to let my biological parents know we would be moving closer to them only to learn that my father had died earlier that day. Barb's father also passed away about six months later.

Although my job title in Charles County remained the same (planning director), I assumed responsibility for a much larger staff. Where I had previously supervised a department of up to twelve at the regional planning commission in Anniston, I was placed in charge of a staff of 26 that grew to 30 before I left for Cumberland late in 2007. The job was very demanding and stressful, as I had to manage the staff's review of roughly 700 active subdivisions, site plans, and building permits. The pace and magnitude of the county's rapid growth and development during that period often seemed overwhelming. Fortunately, I had very good and supportive people to work with who helped me learn the ropes quickly.

Charles County became my first experience living and working near a major city since I attended graduate school in the mid-1980s. The suburban community where we lived, Waldorf, was only 25 miles south of downtown Washington, DC. We eventually learned that our house was located directly beneath the alternate flight path into Washington National Airport whenever changes in wind direction conflicted with the normal approach path. That, in and of itself, was unnerving, but the daily traffic congestion along the few highways leading in and out of the city was truly overwhelming. It took us many months just to overcome the fear of driving in that environment. We had never experienced anything like it.

I remember seeing a two-panel cartoon from the Washington Post that really captured the experience of Washington traffic well. The first panel showed a pioneer couple riding in a horse-drawn carriage down a dirt road leading into Washington. The wife was asking her husband when they would reach the city. His response was, "Well, at this pace, we should get there by dark." The second panel showed a husband and wife sitting in a car that was stranded in a traffic jam on a multi-lane freeway heading into Washington.

The wife's question and the husband's answer were the same. City living during my lifetime had certainly changed.

Another aspect of life in Charles County that made a lasting impression on me was the intense vanity and greed that I witnessed in the general society. The rapid pace of growth, driven by the desperate search for more affordable housing in the Washington area, was driving up land and housing values in Charles County at a remarkable rate. Applications for large subdivisions were being submitted almost daily, and developers were realizing huge profits on speculative lands that they had acquired ten to twenty years earlier. There seemed to be no limit to the potential for development and to the rising market value of the homes that were being built. For example, we purchased an 1,800 square foot house on a 7,500 square foot lot for about $250,000 in November 2004. That same house had been sold in 2000 for about $75,000. By November 2006, when we obtained an equity credit line on the house to purchase our property in Pendleton County, our house was appraised at well over $300,000. It was an unprecedented housing boom that we knew could never be sustainable.

I can recall many examples of the greed and vanity that emerged from that booming economy, but none of them capture it better than a meeting I had with one local developer over an issue he faced in satisfying one of our basic subdivision regulations. The pace of growth and development in Charles County was overwhelming the county's ability to widen and build new roads to manage the increasing traffic congestion. The three counties of southern Maryland (Charles, St. Mary's, and Calvert) are confined to a narrow peninsula of land that falls between the Potomac and Patuxent Rivers. As a result, there were only a few major roads to carry all of the local and commuting traffic. Charles County was working to widen many of its deficient roads and build new roads to address the problem, but managing the public expense of that massive road-building program required more time than the rate of traffic growth would allow.

To deal with this problem, the county imposed a requirement that, wherever feasible, all new subdivisions had to provide (at logical points) road extensions to adjoining properties that were likely to be developed in the near future. The future developer of the neighboring parcel would then be required to extend those dead-end streets into his subdivision so that, over time, new local streets would be built that would provide alternate routes for local traffic to the congested main highways. These new streets between adjoining subdivisions were called "interparcel connections."

One particular subdivision developer was especially unhappy about the county planning staff's insistence that he connect one of the streets in his proposed subdivision with an interparcel connector that had already been built in an adjoining subdivision. He argued with staff so long and hard about the issue that I was finally asked to intervene and resolve the conflict. When I sat down to meet with the applicant and my staff, the developer gave me a list of concerns he had about our request that he connect his proposed street with the existing dead-end street in the neighboring subdivision. His first concern was that the location where he would have to make the connection was too environmentally sensitive. Given the overall development density of his subdivision, it clearly wasn't a valid concern. This same developer had often accused staff of being too protective of the environment, yet he was arguing that we were asking him to destroy an environmentally sensitive area. Once he finally admitted that concern wasn't valid, he tried to argue that the land was too steep to build the required street connection. That, too, was ridiculous, as the distance was very short and the overall change in elevation was less than five feet.

After we had discussed several more similarly outlandish and unjustifiable problems he raised, he finally revealed the real reason why he was objecting to the interparcel connection. He pointed out that the house values in the neighboring subdivision were about $240,000 to $300,000. Then he said that the houses he was planning to build would be valued at between $450,000 and $600,000. Certainly, I could understand, he asserted, why the people who wanted to buy the homes in *his* subdivision would not want the people living in the neighboring subdivision to be driving on their streets. Essentially, he was of the opinion that people who lived in half-million-dollar homes would be offended to find people who live in quarter-million-dollar homes driving on their streets. I responded to his concern by asking him if the people in his subdivision would truly be afraid that I (who could barely afford my own quarter-million dollar-home) might try to steal from them. He thought silently for a moment about what he had said before finally agreeing to build the interparcel connector.

Lifestyle Lost

That sort of snobby attitude was (and presumably still is) prevalent throughout the Washington metropolitan area. I encountered it many times in different situations throughout my experience in Charles County, and it was not unusual to hear about it from my counterparts in other communities. It was also reflected in the architectural style of many newly constructed homes in the area, which I often referred to as "contemporary pretentious." Perhaps someday in the next 50-75 years, historic preservationists will recognize those homes as a distinctive architectural style from that period worthy of preservation. Such is life in a predominantly urban society.

****

By the end of 2005, I was becoming exhausted and stressed out from the demands and pace of our life and frustrated by the lack of integrity evident in the attitudes and actions of the people who set the standards of conduct for our modern society. The influential trend-setting people I interacted with during the course of my daily work were not the role models I was taught to look up to and aspire to become. Most neighbors didn't really socialize with each other; they competed with each other to buy the newest or biggest car or make the most envied and conspicuous improvement to their home or property. Parents contributed to the overwhelming traffic congestion that they complained about by driving their children to school in large part because they were afraid to let their children ride in the school buses that passed before their homes. Some of the parents who did allow their kids to ride the school bus would drive them to the ends of their 75-100 foot driveways to wait for the bus to come, then back their cars into their garages after the bus left. I saw this frivolous and wasteful pattern of behavior many times during my morning commutes to work.

I am always perplexed by the bizarre and inherent contradictions I see between personal behavior and the values that we admire and espouse. For example, we hear frequent news reports and talk about how obese and out-of-shape people have become. The often-cited solution is that we need to live healthier and more active lives. To me, that means we should stop depending on technology to alleviate us of physical labor and dining out at fast food restaurants. My wife and I have made a commitment to grow a garden, cook meals at home from scratch, and build our own retirement home—all of which improve the quality of the food we eat and force us to do useful and meaningful labor.

For many people, though, the solution is to buy into a packaged dietary meal program, buy diet pills, and/or pay for a gym membership so you can spend an hour walking on a treadmill that takes you nowhere. We seem to be so accustomed to buying the solutions to our problems and needs that we don't even consider changing our patterns of behavior in ways that *reduce* our basic dependency on money and technology. People seem to have lost the understanding of what a self-reliant lifestyle is and what it means for our health. It's easier to just buy what society offers as the latest trendy technology or movie-star-endorsed solution.

I also find the commercials that I have recently seen on television to be particularly vain and ludicrous. The one that currently bothers me most is an advertisement for certain income tax consultants who seek to represent delinquent taxpayers. What first caught my attention was the commercial's initial appeal to people that "owe more than $10,000 in back taxes." It seems to me that if you already *know* you owe more than $10,000 in *back* taxes, you already understand that you've violated the law. I can accept that *some* people may occasionally make honest mistakes and may not realize them until it's too late, but I find it hard to casually accept that it happens by accident frequently enough to justify the cost of a national television ad campaign.

The firm then touts the services of its former IRS professionals who can help you defeat the IRS' efforts to collect the back taxes and penalties that you owe. Excuse me, my wife and I may not like having to pay taxes, but we have always paid what we honestly owe. Why should I feel that this company is providing a valuable service to our society by helping people who know they haven't paid their taxes avoid penalties for not having paid *their* fair share of the cost of our government? It seems to me that every time they successfully help a tax evader escape paying taxes it only increases the cost burden of operating our government on the honest taxpayers. I always fuss about this commercial whenever I see it on television. I guess the subtle message I should take from these commercials is that we shouldn't have to worry about the repercussions from evading our income taxes. How does this jibe with our core American values?

Unfortunately, not even the shameful audacity of high-priced tax consultants selling their services to delinquent taxpayers can overshadow the gross abuse of our increasingly limited tax resources to the extent that I have seen from one specific industry—Industrial Wind Energy. From what I have learned over the past four years, it is a story that deserves far more public attention and scrutiny.

****

I didn't begin to think critically about the merits of wind energy until late 2006, when I started considering how I was going to power the retirement home we planned to build in Pendleton County. I knew that I wanted to minimize our fixed costs of living and our dependency on outside services, so I naturally began looking into solar and wind energy as potential strategies to achieve energy independence. Industrial scale wind energy first came to my attention during our initial exploratory trips into West Virginia earlier that year, as we began searching for retirement property.   At that time, the Mountaineer wind energy project on Backbone Mountain north of Thomas, WV was in full operation. We saw it for the first time during our trips to Blackwater Falls Canyon and Canaan Valley.

Like most people, we found ourselves initially mesmerized by the massive blades rotating slowly atop giant towers strung out along the ridgeline. The immense scale of these projects is quite shocking to those who have never seen them before. Granted, the turbine blades don't operate all the time, but as often as we'd see them spinning it seemed like a good way to utilize a free resource to generate electricity. Perhaps it would make sense to consider using it and/or solar energy to power our retirement home off the electric grid and achieve energy independence. What could be a better way to live a self-reliant lifestyle than to power your home with an unlimited, free power source and eliminate a utility bill that would be controlled by someone else?

When I was in elementary school, our science class conducted a science fair. All students had to create a project or display for the fair as part of our grade for the class. I decided to demonstrate how solar power worked. To prepare for the project, my father and I visited a couple of people he knew in southern Vermont who were using solar energy indirectly to help heat their homes and reduce their electric demand to produce hot water.

The homes we visited were specifically designed with large, south-facing, thermal-pane windows that allowed more light to shine into the house in the winter months than during summer. The homeowners had also designed homemade solar panel boxes containing Plexiglass or fiberglass covers and an internal network of water pipes. The pipes and backing in each box were painted flat black. These panel boxes were mounted on the roofs of each home and were connected directly into the water supply lines that fed into the hot water tanks.

Sunlight shining on the panel boxes would heat the water as it was pumped from the pressure tank into the hot water tank. By preheating the water before it refilled the hot water tank, the system reduced the amount of electricity the hot water tank would draw to raise the water temperature to the desired level. This type of system is known as a passive solar energy approach, and it's a less intensive or efficient way of tapping the sun's energy than I am contemplating for our retirement home. However, back in the early to mid-1970s, we considered those models to be state-of-the-art systems.

To demonstrate this water heating concept, I constructed a corrugated cardboard house with a miniature solar panel box on the roof that had black plastic (the material we used in our garden to grow tomatoes) mounted on the back of the panel box. I ran a line of clear plastic surgical tubing through the panel box and forced water into it using a hand operated bulb pump. I installed a water reservoir tank on one side of the house and a heated water storage tank on the other side. Both tanks were equipped with mercury thermometers to show the before and after water temperatures. I used a strong ultraviolet lamp (which we used to start our spring vegetable seeds) to represent the sun. By slowly pumping water from the storage reservoir through the solar panel box and into the receiving tank, I was able to produce a three-to-five degree increase in water temperature.

It wasn't a powerful demonstration, but it did spark my interest in the potential for alternative energy use, and I have followed it periodically ever since. I really had little knowledge of wind energy, but it certainly didn't *seem* as complicated. That was a false assumption which you may begin to understand when I try to explain how it really works.

Based on my basic understanding of alternative energy that I accumulated over the years, I fully realized that we would have to make some major lifestyle adjustments to live in a home powered exclusively by wind or solar energy. For example, you can't expect wind or solar energy to be available whenever you want it. Appliances that demand a lot of electricity, such as an electric oven and a clothes dryer, can't be used simultaneously because you won't have access to unlimited volumes of electricity. Although you can use batteries to store electricity produced by a wind turbine or solar panels at a residential scale, you still have to budget your electricity needs to survive through extended periods of time when the wind doesn't blow or the sun doesn't shine enough.

One way to overcome this problem is to use redundant technologies to help manage our electricity demand. For example, we decided that we could use an old-fashioned wood-fired cookstove, like the one we had when I was growing up, to both heat the house in the winter time and cook our meals. That would allow us to avoid using an electric stove or microwave oven during a time of the year when solar panels would produce less electricity. We could also use a liquid propane gas generator to recharge the batteries when wind or solar energy couldn't keep pace with our demand for electricity. These seemed like reasonable accommodations, although I discovered that the generator I would need would be large and expensive, and LP gas is one of the more expensive fuel sources relative to the electricity I could produce with it. Still, the thought of true energy independence was inescapably alluring to me.

I also realized that I would need to purchase some additional, and quite expensive, equipment to power our basic appliances with wind or solar energy. Most standard appliances and electrical systems are designed to operate using alternating current (AC) electrical service. Wind turbines and solar panels generate direct current (DC) electricity. In order to utilize DC electricity to power an AC system or appliances, you must install a device commonly known as an inverter to convert the DC power into AC. It is possible to buy some appliances that can use DC power directly, but they tend to be very expensive and hard to find. They also tend to be less powerful and effective than appliances powered by alternating current. Furthermore, it is necessary to make sure that *everything* you intend to power is designed for DC power (not just the major appliances) if you hope to avoid purchasing an inverter.

Using an inverter to integrate DC power into an AC system is also beneficial if there is a chance that you might have to sell your house in the future. Your buyer's market might be very limited if the future owners can't easily and quickly reconvert your energy supply to standard AC power. Most people will not choose to make the lifestyle sacrifices that we were willing to make. All things considered, purchasing an inverter and wiring the house to accept either AC or DC power makes a lot more sense for the overall high investment expense.

You also need special batteries and a *lot* of them. Some people have used standard car batteries to store residential scale solar or wind energy, but they aren't designed for heavy power drains. You really need a special type of battery known as a deep cycle battery that can withstand heavy drains and complete recharging. Even so, their useful lifespan can vary between five and ten years. Consequently, you have to consider replacement costs for the batteries, in addition to the cost of maintaining your electrical generating equipment (solar panels or wind turbine).

In some cases, you still need to make sure that your appliances can operate under the amperage constraints of your specific solar panels or wind turbine. Depending on the generating strength of your electrical system, you may have to purchase special appliances, especially for those appliances that draw heavy electrical loads, such as an electric oven, clothes dryer, or a hot water heater. In reality, there are a lot of cost and energy use considerations that need to be made to take advantage of either wind or solar energy.

When I investigated the cost of the basic wind or solar generating systems, the initial investment costs for both were comparable at about $30,000-$35,000. Equipment dealers will quickly point out that some of these up-front costs can be offset to some degree by special energy tax credits and future energy cost savings, which they generally said would pay back the initial investment cost in about 25-30 years.

However, I realized that the alleged energy cost recovery schedules I was given did not include routine maintenance costs that must be absorbed over the 25-30 year payback period. The batteries become a fixed cost for either basic system, wind or solar. Assuming a 5-10 year useful lifespan under either energy scenario, one must expect to replace them between two and six times during the entire payback period—a significant periodic expense. However, there is also an ongoing routine maintenance expense for the basic generating equipment. This expense differs greatly between solar and wind energy.

Solar panels are typically low maintenance energy generating devices. They are vulnerable to three specific threats that can affect their performance—dust and debris accumulation, snow cover, and hail. Hail can damage the panels; however, most solar panels are designed to withstand significant hail impact and can have useful warrantied lifespans of up to 50 years. Over time the panels will collect dust, which reduces their ability to capture solar radiation. They also must be cleaned after snowstorms. If the panels are mounted on the roof of the house, this maintenance work can be challenging, especially for older people. However, solar panels can be mounted on the ground to make it easier for such routine cleaning and washing work.

Wind turbines, on the other hand, pose significant routine maintenance challenges for the owner. To capture the best winds, the turbines must be elevated between 65 and 150 feet above the ground—depending on local site conditions. That is, of course, assuming that the prevailing wind speeds and exposure are conducive to generating useful electricity. This is often the biggest impediment for most homes. In addition, the high elevation of the turbine and the need for extensive routine services (cleaning the blades to keep them in proper balance, lubricating the turbine equipment, and replacing critical parts) can be difficult, if not impossible, for the owner to do by him/herself. In most cases, a long-term maintenance contract is needed to ensure that the turbine operates efficiently and can be repaired when a problem occurs. This is a significant on-going cost that can be avoided with solar energy. It also adds to the additional costs that must be assumed throughout the overall payback period that makes wind energy more costly to afford over the long term.

I also evaluated the energy production rates for both wind and solar energy. I had expected solar energy to be far more efficient in the southern and western states, where the typically arid climate provides more clear days than is common in the northeast. Our area in West Virginia is also exposed to higher winds in the winter months, which made me assume that wind energy would be far more efficient in that regard than solar. However, that assumption proved incorrect.

Frostburg State University, about twelve miles west of Cumberland, MD, has a renewable energy research program. They adapted a building the size of a typical house to be powered by both solar panels and a small wind turbine. They monitored the amount of electricity that each system produced over the course of a year (September 1, 2007 through August 31, 2008). Since the two systems produced slightly different levels of electricity, they weighted the electrical outputs generated by each system to reflect what they would have generated if they had identical generation capacities.

The results that they obtained showed that the solar panels generated significantly more electricity than the wind turbine during eight months of the year. Only during the three windiest winter months, December through February, did the wind turbine produce more electricity than the solar panels. In fact, the data showed that during the months of April through October (a 7-month period), the solar panels produced more than three times as much electricity as the wind turbine. The resulting report concluded, under the local climatic conditions, that the solar panels had an overall potential payback period of less than 25 years, as opposed to roughly 25 years or more for the wind turbine.[iv] Again, those payback schedules did not account for maintenance costs and routine battery replacement.

This information and the overall results of my initial investigation into residential scale wind and solar energy convinced me that on the basis of initial and long-term costs, ease of maintenance, and electrical generating potential, solar power was consistently superior to wind energy. This finding was even true for homes in the predominantly cloudy and windy mid-Atlantic region of the Appalachian Mountains. Ever since I completed this investigation, I have focused on solar energy as my primary choice for off-grid electricity. Virtually all of the people I have met in our area who are using alternative energy sources have also chosen solar power. Given this situation, I began to wonder why such huge industrial wind energy projects like the Mountaineer project near Thomas, WV were the predominant new source of alternative commercial energy being developed in our immediate area. What I eventually learned about it only reinforced the concerns I have raised regarding the lack of integrity in our basic economic system.

****

To fully understand the problems I have come to know about industrial wind energy projects, it is necessary to learn more details about how they operate and how they interact with the electrical grid than is commonly known. In order to provide that understanding, I must explain in great detail what I learned through my professional work. Given the highly technical nature of these issues, I will do my best to explain it as simply and succinctly as I can. Please bear in mind that will not be an easy task.

One of the earliest assignments I received after becoming the Cumberland city planner was to evaluate the impacts of industrial wind energy and determine what, if any, new regulations the city might need to consider to manage them. The issue was raised by a proposal for a new large industrial wind energy project consisting of more than twenty turbines spread out along Dan's Mountain, the tallest and most prominent ridgeline in the state of Maryland. The project would be clearly visible from Cumberland, and the city had additional ridgelines within its borders that could be considered for other industrial scale projects. The city was concerned about how this new form of development should be addressed. This assignment gave me an opportunity to more thoroughly evaluate industrial scale wind energy and how it works.

It is quite easy to believe that industrial wind turbines produce useful and reliable volumes of electricity. People who pass by or see these massive turbines routinely see the blades spinning slowly most of the time. As a result, it is understandably difficult to accept that industrial wind turbines are one of the least efficient (if not the outright least efficient) modes of commercial energy production contributing electricity to the grid. To understand how that can be, it is important to learn how they work.

Industrial wind turbines generate electricity whenever the wind turns the blades. Each turbine has a maximum rated output of electricity that it can produce, if the wind speeds fall within a specific range. This maximum output is called the turbine's *rated* or *nameplate capacity*, and is usually measured in megawatts of electricity produced over a one-hour period (commonly referred to as megawatt hours—MWh). The wind speeds that are necessary to achieve this maximum production are generally between 36 and 55 MPH. Sustained wind speeds above that range can cause the turbine to overload and burn out. In some cases, the turbines can explode or break apart from component fatigue and/or overheating of the turbine. When a threat of excessive winds (56 MPH or greater) is forecasted, the turbines must be shut down to protect them from damage either by braking the blades and/or turning the blades so they don't face the wind.

Likewise, if the winds are not blowing hard enough, they lack the force needed to make the massive blades rotate or they rotate too slowly to produce any measurable amount of electricity. Consequently, the turbines will not produce any electricity if the wind speeds fall below seven miles per hour for any extended period of time, depending on the model. If a turbine's blades are rotating when the winds are blowing less than this threshold speed, then it is likely that they are being powered by *drawing* electricity from the grid.

Some industrial wind turbines are designed to use electricity to power the blades during extended periods of low winds, so that they are ready to begin producing electricity again as soon as the wind speeds increase to or only slightly above their operational threshold level. If the blades aren't already turning when the wind speed reaches this threshold level, they may have to wait for a stronger gust to break the inertia of the heavy blades and get them started. By powering the blades, they can help the turbines capture lower wind speeds and begin producing electricity again. The price of that opportunity is that the overall *net* volume of electricity they can produce is reduced by the amount of electricity the turbines must consume to power the blades.

When prevailing wind speeds fall within the range of seven and fifty-five MPH, most industrial wind turbines will produce electricity. However, the actual amount of electricity they can produce varies greatly with small changes in the wind speed. In fact, this variability in electrical output is far greater than the relative change in wind speed that causes it. That is because the primary factor that determines how much electricity a wind turbine can produce is the wind speed cubed (multiplied by itself three times).[v]

To understand how this factor affects the power output of a wind turbine, it is easier to think of the maximum electricity a turbine can produce at optimum wind speeds (at least 36 MPH) as a gallon of water. If the prevailing wind speeds were to suddenly decrease by half that threshold to eighteen MPH, the actual amount of electricity the turbine could produce would be one pint (1/8 of a gallon). If the relationship between wind speed and power output were one-to-one, then a reduction in wind speed by one-half would produce one-half of the turbine's potential output. Since the actual relationship between wind speed and output is *exponential* rather than direct, the actual output is only one-quarter of the amount that you would normally expect to receive, if the relationship was one-to-one. If the wind speed is reduced again by one-half to nine MPH, the turbine would produce only ¼ cup of electricity, which is only 1/64th of the turbine's maximum output.

When you compare the ¼ cup of electricity to the full gallon of electricity that the turbine is *capable* of producing, you can see why the actual electrical output from a wind turbine is so highly variable. Average wind speeds (particularly over land) vary greatly over very short periods of time. It would take gale-force winds sustained over the course of an entire year for an industrial wind turbine to produce and sustain its maximum potential output. Does that ever occur where you live? Once the wind speeds begin to vary even slightly, the electrical output will vary by many times the actual change in wind speeds.

When industrial wind energy project developers say that their project is *capable* of powering tens of thousands of homes, they are usually basing that figure on the maximum rated capacity. In other words, they are telling you how many homes their turbines can power if the wind blows constantly between 36 and 55 MPH throughout the entire year. In fact, most land-based industrial wind turbines operating today actually produce somewhere between 20% and 30% (depending on local conditions) of the actual electricity they are *capable* of producing (their maximum output) over any average year. Furthermore, fully 20% of the time they will produce no electricity, due to wind speeds that fall outside their productive range—and a good portion of that time the turbines may actually be *consuming* electricity from the grid rather than producing power to keep the heavy rotor blades spinning. During those extended periods of time when an array of giant industrial wind turbines is incapable of producing electricity, they could not even power a six-volt flashlight. Do you want the lights in your house to go on when you flip the switch or only when the wind is blowing at the right speed? No land-based industrial wind energy project has *ever* produced its maximum energy output for a full month, much less a full year.

So why do industrial wind energy developers make such exaggerated statements based on their *potential* energy production when they know it could never really be achieved and then fail to mention all of these limitations on what they can produce? It's because they, like many business and political interests, are *marketing* their product. They want you to support their projects so they can build them and profit from them regardless of whether or not they can deliver what is promised. Is that really too unusual to expect?

It is important to understand that truth-telling in marketing is highly selective. Marketing, as it is commonly practiced, is the art of taking the *whole* truth about a product, service, or issue and strategically dividing it into the "advantageous truth" and the "inconvenient truth." The advantageous truth is the truth (which is often exaggerated) about the product, service, or issue that makes it very attractive to the consumer. The inconvenient truth is the truth about the product, service, or issue that might make it unattractive to the consumer. The truth you promote and advertise about the product, service, or issue is the advantageous truth. The inconvenient truth is left to the consumer to figure out on his/her own. This approach to marketing appears to have become a standard practice in all aspects of society. In the political world, it is referred to as "political spin doctoring," but it follows the same basic principles (if you can call them that). Why else would you hear people say "buyer beware" so often?

These marketing practices are so well accepted and profitable that it says a great deal to me about the relative value of profit versus ethical integrity to our modern society. However, it is not just the fact that the actual electrical output from industrial wind turbines is so variable that makes its electricity practically worthless to the electric grid, it's the fact that it varies so wildly and unpredictably over brief periods of time. Electricity consumers want reliable, consistent electrical supplies, and the people who manage the electrical grid need electrical producers that can control their output on demand. As you will see, the fact that industrial wind turbines are incapable of satisfying these most basic needs is their greatest overall weakness.

Not all electrical power generators have equal production value when they are connected to the regional grid. The electrical grid is not simply one uniform national grid, but an interconnected series of smaller and locally managed regional grids that are powered by different combinations of electricity suppliers. Plants capable of generating large volumes of electricity that are stable and reliable over time and are capable of being increased or decreased on call to serve fluctuations in power demand are highly valued as electricity suppliers. This is because they can produce electricity that satisfies all the basic aspects of demand on the grid. For these reasons, they are deemed to have high capacity value to provide useful electricity for the grid.

A supplier's "capacity value" is the average percentage of a plant's rated or nameplate capacity that can be reasonably expected to be available for use on the grid during any random fifteen-minute period. A plant's capacity value is enhanced if the cost of producing electricity is relatively low, which helps manage consumer prices at competitive levels. It is further enhanced if the source is located close to the major sources of demand, which minimizes the gradual loss of electricity that results when line resistance from transmission over great distances converts a portion of the voltage into heat. Sources of electricity with the highest capacity values and lowest average costs are prioritized to serve the most basic and constant demand on the grid (known in the industry as "baseload demand").

Sources of electricity that fluctuate or vary over time have limited reliability to serve essential or baseload demand on the grid. The grid's ability to provide reliable electricity depends on reliable and controllable supplies of power to maintain a delicate balance between active supplies and demand. If the supply of electricity on the grid falls below demand, even for a brief period of time, a brownout or blackout will occur. If the supply of electricity on the grid surges above demand, damage can occur to plant equipment, resulting in a catastrophic production failure or a blackout.

A good analogy to understand the importance of energy supply stability and balance on the grid is to compare it with the human cardiovascular system. The heart is the critical generator that keeps oxygen-rich blood flowing through the arteries and veins that extend throughout our bodies, just as the active energy generators on the grid keep electricity flowing through the power transmission lines. Both our hearts and our electrical system function by a form of "alternating current."

In the human body, oxygen-rich blood is pumped from the left ventricle of the heart into all parts of the body and returns to the right ventricle to be reoxygenated before being recycled again. When a person is at rest, the heart completes an average of 60-100 beats (cycles) per minute, depending to a large degree on the age and physical condition of the person. An infant's heartbeat can be as high as 120 or more beats per minute, which reduces gradually with age.

Electric power on the energy grid similarly "cycles" or alternates between positive and negative charges at roughly 60 cycles per second or hertz (Hz). This is the standard cycle frequency for the electric grid when the balance between energy production and energy demand is balanced or "stable."

When a person exercises intensely or works hard, the body 's heartbeat or heart rate will increase to provide the extra oxygen and blood flow the body needs to undertake intense physical activity. The increased heart rate causes the body's blood pressure to increase accordingly. If the increased heart rate and the resulting high blood pressure level is continued for a long period of time, the potential for a heart attack and death also increases. Alternatively, if a person's heart rate and blood pressure declines too rapidly, as occurs when an artery is severed, the person will lose consciousness and, if the condition persists, die. This all makes sense to you because it is common knowledge.

However, the same situation can occur on the electric grid when the standard frequency of alternating current on the grid fluctuates above or below the 60-hertz rated frequency of most devices and machines powered by electricity. The frequency of the grid can drop below 60 hertz when energy demand increases rapidly and unexpectedly (relative to the available supply of electricity on the grid to satisfy it), as can and does occur when a sudden heat wave or a cold wave causes a periodic spike in electrical demand for heating or cooling. The result under this condition— as many people know from experience—is a brownout or, if the condition persists too long, a blackout.

On the other hand, an unexpected surge of electricity on the grid from suppliers when overall electrical demand is stable or dropping will cause the frequency of the alternating current on the grid to spike above 60 hertz, resulting in the overloading and burnout of devices connected to the grid and/or a power blackout. The resulting consequences of rapidly fluctuating power and demand on the electric grid are virtually identical to the effects of rapidly fluctuating blood pressure on the human body. As a result, a delicate balance between supply and demand on the grid must always be maintained to sustain the grid and provide the dependable electricity that consumers demand.

The greater the variability of electrical production (especially if it occurs over short periods of time), the less reliable a source may be to serve baseload demand and the greater the potential for brownouts or blackouts to occur, especially if demand on the grid fluctuates suddenly. Those sources that are not "dispatchable," or able to increase or decrease production when called upon to do so, have even less ability to satisfy periodic peak demands.   Inherently unstable forms of electrical production must be supplemented in some way by a more reliable or dispatchable form of power to reduce or compensate for output fluctuations. This means that energy suppliers that are not dispatchable (like all wind energy systems) must use some form of electrical storage system or they must be backed up (balanced) by more dispatchable suppliers already actively powering the grid or by special supporting generators (peaking generators) at the integration point to minimize or reduce potential instability in the supply of electricity on the grid.

Industrial wind energy, like all other sources of industrial electricity serving the grid, must be evaluated against these industry criteria. Overall, industrial wind energy turbines have very low capacity value and cannot provide reliable and dispatchable volumes of electricity when called upon to do so during peak demand periods. These low values for industrial wind energy are due to high and unpredictable variability in electrical output over short time periods, low average output, inability to ramp production up or down on demand, and locational constraints that often place them at considerable distances from sources of demand. The relatively high unit production cost of industrial wind only reduces its overall value and utility to the grid as a marketable source of electricity. These constraints make it extremely difficult for industrial wind energy to effectively serve as a baseload generator of commercial electricity or as a marginal reserve to serve periodic spikes in demand.

Even at relatively low levels of integration, industrial wind energy can pose a concern for grid stability. Its volatility in production over short time intervals makes it difficult for grid managers to maintain reliable supplies of electricity at a stable frequency on the grid. These fluctuations in production become an additional factor that must be finely balanced with periodic fluctuations in demand. Grid managers have managed to introduce industrial wind projects into the grid, as long as the volume of wind energy is relatively low, more reliable back-up generation is available, and/or sufficient marginal reserves of electricity can be called upon to offset the inherent fluctuations in wind energy production. Nevertheless, grid managers often raise concerns about the impacts of fluctuating industrial wind energy production on specific transmission corridors or lines, where sufficient capacity and controls do not exist to maintain stability over time. These concerns raise serious fundamental questions about the potential impacts of large-scale integration of wind energy into the grid and the levels at which potential fluctuations in wind energy production pose a threat to grid stability. The level of power instability that the grid can accommodate is likely to vary greatly in different regions of the national electric grid and at different times, based on variations in local supplies of and demand for electricity.

In fact, even with the currently low level of grid integration that exists today, at least two recent incidents have occurred in the United States where industrial wind energy has caused serious grid instability. The first occurred in Texas on February 27, 2008 when production from wind energy projects on the grid unexpectedly dropped by 1,400 megawatts. The loss of scheduled electricity contributed to a stage two emergency, which forced grid operators to reduce service to interruptible power customers for approximately 90 minutes until adequate supplies (from other sources) could be restored.[vi] The Texas regional grid has one of the highest volumes of installed wind energy capacity in the U.S.

A second incident occurred in the Columbia River Gorge during June 2009, when electrical output from a large series of wind turbines unexpectedly shot up by 1,000 megawatts and then plummeted by nearly the same amount in less than an hour. The dramatic variation in output forced the Bonneville Power Administration to quickly ramp up and down output from a series of hydro-electric dams to keep the grid in balance.[vii] As more industrial wind turbines are integrated into the grid, the capacity to suddenly increase or decrease output from other dispatchable supplies will need to be increased significantly in order to maintain grid stability and avoid power interruption emergencies like the 2008 incident that occurred in the Texas grid.

The logical and simple solution to this problem would be to connect the wind turbines to batteries that can store the electricity they produce and release it to the grid over time to even out the production. This solution is commonly used for residential scale wind energy, but its application to large industrial wind energy projects poses a significant and costly problem. The use of lithium battery technology has proven to be more difficult for industrial wind projects because the extreme variations in electrical output can cause overheating and excessive wear and tear on the batteries. In some instances, project developers have proposed to install batteries that are charged from the grid, which provides the stable flows of electricity that the turbines can't. However, this strategy only adds to the demand for electricity from the grid and further reduces the effective net production of the wind turbines. It also raises the question of how industrial wind energy can be a stable and useful supply of energy to the grid if it can't even be used to recharge its own back-up batteries.

In other instances, industrial wind energy projects have been paired with both non-greenhouse and greenhouse gas emitting energy producers in the same local grid service area to help balance out fluctuations in industrial wind energy production. These co-generation scenarios have utilized a wide range of supporting producers from coal-fired plants to hydroelectric facilities (as in the Columbia River Gorge).

When paired with coal-fired plants, the need to ramp production up and down over brief periods of time in response to co-generated wind energy fluctuations can lead to gross inefficiencies in production for the coal-fired plants, resulting in *increased* greenhouse gas emissions. In order to ramp down (reduce) production in response to an unexpected surge in wind energy production, a coal plant must vent steam that has already been produced from the burning of coal, resulting in lower production efficiency and output. The effect is the same as a steam engine stopping at a railroad station. A steam train engine does not stop by reducing its rate of coal consumption; it does so by venting steam pressure already produced by the burning of coal. Once coal has been burned to produce steam, venting the steam does not eliminate the carbon emissions that have already been released. It only means that no benefit was received from steam that was produced from the original carbon emission. Coal fuel consumption (and the resulting greenhouse gas emissions that the burning of coal produces) can only be reduced where a decrease in demand is consistent over long periods of time, which cannot be assured or controlled by unpredictable industrial wind energy production.

Similar production inefficiencies can occur when industrial wind energy projects are paired with hydro-electric projects (as illustrated by the June 2009 Columbia River Gorge incident). In order to retain generating capacity to increase production when industrial wind energy output drops unexpectedly, a hydro-electric plant must withhold productive capacity as a potential spinning (or standby) reserve. Consequently, the impact of an industrial wind energy project can be to offset or reduce clean hydroelectric energy production from a co-generating plant rather than displacing electricity from a greenhouse gas generating source.

Pairing industrial wind energy projects with hydro-electric plants can also raise additional critical service and resource management issues. Most major hydro-electric facilities must balance their electricity production against other competing uses and water demands. These competing uses and demands can include downstream flood management, storage of essential drinking water supplies, and maintaining water levels for water-based transportation and shipping. The need to suddenly increase hydro-electric production by releasing large volumes of water to balance out a sudden drop in co-generated wind energy can cause serious policy dilemmas for projects designed to store safe drinking water reserves in periods of severe drought or retain downstream floodwaters in periods of flooding.

Another strategy that has been proffered to mitigate the impacts of wind energy production variability is to distribute wind energy projects over a larger area. This concept is based on the theory that winds blowing at productive speeds in one area can balance or cancel out a sudden decline in production by a wind energy project in another area. Of course, this theory overlooks the problem of electrical energy heat loss resulting from transmission over great distances, but that fact is not the primary problem with it. The theory is premised, in large part, on the mathematical principle that opposing sine waves will cancel out each other. However, this concept presumes that the opposing sine waves have identical amplitudes and frequencies, but opposite and perfectly timed phases so that the peak of one sine wave can precisely offset the valley (low point) of the other. Consequently, this scenario presumes some measure of control over the various production curves that simply cannot be assured through industrial wind energy production. I realize this may be a difficult concept to grasp, but there is an easier way to think about it.

The technical problems of applying this distributive production concept to industrial wind energy can be illustrated, tested, and understood through a simple thought experiment. Imagine three people (each representing a different wind energy project) standing on opposing sides of a large puddle of water. Each person is given a handful of stones that represents the electricity they can produce. The puddle represents the supply of electricity that exists on the electric grid. All three persons are then asked to contribute electricity into the grid by tossing their stones randomly into the puddle, just as wind turbines randomly produce power when the wind blows. The resulting ripples on the surface of the puddle have peaks and valleys that simulate the fluctuations in energy output typically produced by wind turbines.

Under the principle of offsetting sine waves, pebbles of exactly the same size thrown into the puddle with exactly the same force and with perfect timing (so that they can produce waves with opposing phases) will cancel out each other where the waves meet and interact. However, without any assurance that these complex conditions can be controlled or satisfied, there is no way to ensure that the ripples (or electric outputs from the wind energy projects) that are produced will effectively balance out or offset each other. In virtually all scenarios where these essential controls are not present, the resulting ripples will cause greater, not less, water instability or turbulence where they meet in the puddle.

When multiple industrial wind energy projects are integrated into the electric grid over a large area, the ability to effectively control production in a way that will provide the desired balance in power production is simply not possible. Each project will contribute variable volumes of electricity into the grid at unpredictable times and over different intervals in time in response to local wind speeds. Furthermore, since local demand for electricity within the grid varies significantly from one region to another and a delicate balance between supplies and demand must be maintained at all times, electricity produced in one part of the grid simply may not be available to serve demand in another when it is needed.

It is also important to recognize that ambient wind speeds throughout the country generally favor low wind conditions over optimal wind speeds. As a result, industrial wind energy projects everywhere are far more likely to produce low electrical outputs than high outputs at any given point in time. How often and long do winds in any part of the country remain steady at speeds of 36-55 MPH as opposed to 0-8 MPH? This situation results in far more and longer production deficits to offset across the grid than production peaks to effectively compensate for them. As more wind energy projects are integrated into the grid, far more and longer periods of low production will be generated than periods of peak production—a fact clearly illustrated by actual wind production curves.[viii] These and other factors affecting the nature and volume of electricity (none of which can be controlled by grid or project managers) make it virtually impossible that the theory could ever provide any rational compensating benefit for wind energy induced grid instability.

All of these effects highlight the overwhelming complexities and problems involved in utilizing an inherently uncontrollable, non-baseload electrical generator like industrial wind to supplement, displace, or replace electricity generated by a controllable baseload generator, such as coal, nuclear, or hydro-electric power plants. Technological limitations on the grid to effectively integrate or compensate for unstable electrical generators also raise questions about the basic ability of industrial wind turbines to provide useful electricity. It is exceedingly difficult, especially at times and in locations where peak demand for electricity on the grid approaches capacity, to determine or even estimate what level of penetration from industrial wind energy supplies can be safely and successfully integrated into the grid. The actual answer also may vary over time and over distance.

These problems further demonstrate the technical difficulties in achieving meaningful or even credibly documentable greenhouse gas emission reduction benefits from industrial wind energy. I have heard informed observers call industrial wind energy the "ethanol of electrical energy production,"[ix] because it is just as incapable of reducing greenhouse gases as ethanol is now widely accepted to be. Proponents of industrial wind energy simply have not been forced or challenged to present the objective, scientific evidence or facts to support their claims. I'd be willing to bet any amount of money that they can't. You don't have to take my word for it. Simply do the research and critical thinking on your own. When have you ever heard an industrial wind energy project developer or proponent encourage you to thoroughly and objectively research the science of industrial wind? Perhaps there is a good reason why.

Based on this assessment and understanding, I wrote, and the city adopted, zoning regulations for wind energy systems that prohibit industrial-scale wind turbines, but allow smaller residential-scale wind turbines with approval by the board of zoning appeals. The overall poor power production potential from an array of huge, expensive industrial turbines (which requires between three and four acres of forest clearing for each turbine) simply cannot justify or offset the potential environmental and aesthetic impacts on the city's sensitive ridgelines.

****

So, if industrial wind energy cannot produce useful electricity and cannot fulfill its promise to effectively displace coal-fired plants or reduce greenhouse gas emissions, why are so many projects being built? Perhaps it is because of the massive federal government tax subsidies available to developers of industrial wind energy projects and the renewable energy portfolio requirements that are being adopted by many states. The only thing I can determine to be green about industrial wind energy is the money that it brings to its investors. That also appears to be what its developers are chasing.

Industrial wind energy developers have lobbied hard in congress over the years to extend and expand energy production tax credits and other grants and subsidies to offset the high investment costs of their projects. In fact, most project developers freely admit that, without these massive and continuing government subsidies, industrial wind energy development would virtually cease. While it is true that industrial wind receives less total or overall government support than other energy producers, including coal and oil, it is *only* because Industrial Wind Energy is producing so little electricity. When the cost of government subsidies per megawatt hour of electricity generated to the grid is calculated for each source of electrical production, a far different picture emerges.

As documented in an April 2008 federal report, the total government subsidy per megawatt hour of electricity produced by industrial wind energy projects in 2007 was $23.37. This figure compares to only $0.44 per megawatt hour for coal, $0.25 for natural and LP gas, and $0.67 for hydroelectric power.[x] If wind energy is truly as inexpensive and cost effective as the industry would have you believe, then why do they need special laws (cap and trade legislation and renewable energy portfolio standards) and big, ongoing taxpayer subsidies (construction grants and energy production tax credits) to make it feasible? Furthermore, if wind energy requires such huge production subsidies, how affordable do you think the electricity it generates will be and what might that do to your future electric rates—especially if these subsidies are discontinued in the future?

When Congress and the Obama Administration approved federal economic stimulus funds in 2008-2009, industrial wind energy projects benefited even more. According to a White House briefing memo issued to President Obama on October 25, 2010, with the combination of Section 1705 Energy Loan Guaranties and Section 1603 grants and a favorable capital depreciation schedule, wind energy developers can reduce their costs for capital development to as low as 11% of the project cost, even though they would receive an estimated return on investment of about 30%. The memo also estimates that average government subsidies for wind energy development now constitute approximately 65% of the total project cost.[xi]

If the prospect of greatly reduced capital investment costs isn't enough to entice energy companies to invest in wind energy, then federal energy production tax credits, which provide generous tax subsidies for electricity generated from wind and solar, help to sweeten the pot. The tax credits for wind energy helped entice Florida Power and Light, which generates most of its energy from coal-fired plants, to make huge investments in industrial wind energy development. The tax credits they receive from their combined industrial wind energy investments have helped them eliminate paying any corporate taxes to the federal government for several years. According to an October 7, 2007 report in the Palm Beach News Post, "FPL Energy [a subsidiary of Florida Power and Light Company] boasted a 2006 profit of $610 million, triple its earnings in 2005. That followed an earnings increase of 200 percent between 1998 and 2002, then significant profit growth each year thereafter, mostly fueled by wind power projects."[xii]

As reported by ABC World News on March 25, 2011, General Electric earned $14.2 billion in corporate profits in 2010, but paid *no* income taxes to the federal government. Much of the write-off was blamed on losses incurred by its financial arm, GE Capital, during the financial meltdown. However, White House spokesperson, Jay Carney, noted that GE hires legions of corporate attorneys who know how to take advantage of tax loopholes.[xiii] Need I note that GE is also heavily invested in developing industrial wind energy technology?

A prime current example of the extreme taxpayer subsidies involved in industrial wind energy development is the Shepherds Flat project in Oregon that is being financed, in part, by General Electric—the same company that paid no income taxes to the federal Government in 2010. The U.S. Department of Energy is subsidizing the $1.9 billion project in the form of a $1.06 billion government loan guaranty. Furthermore, as soon as the project begins producing electricity, the developers will receive a cash grant of $490 million from the U.S. Treasury Department.[xiv]

Consider all of these little ironies. Industrial wind energy cannot produce electricity that can effectively substitute for or displace electricity produced from coal-fired plants, but it does make coal-fired plants on the grid operate less efficiently so that they emit *more* carbon dioxide. In addition, lucrative federal tax subsidies to promote industrial wind energy development can be tapped by companies that produce electricity from coal making them more profitable and helping them reduce their tax liabilities. Industrial wind energy cannot produce the reliable electricity we need to make the grid less vulnerable to blackouts; its highly variable production over short periods in time actually contributes to grid instability and potential blackouts. While industrial wind energy utilizes a free natural resource—the wind—to produce electricity, it represents one of the most (if not *the* most) expensive sources of electricity per megawatt hour of electricity produced on the grid to *both* the taxpayer and the ratepayer. How do these inconvenient truths promote clean energy and achieve promised reductions in greenhouse gas emissions? Is this really how our increasingly scarce tax dollars should be spent?

Federal (taxpayer-funded) subsidies virtually eliminate any investment risk to private developers seeking to construct industrial wind energy projects. In essence, the taxpayers are footing the bill, so why not develop the project whether it works as promised or not? The risk that these government subsidies could be discontinued at any time (perhaps when the public catches on and demands that they be discontinued) may also help explain why the vast majority of all wind energy projects are developed by Limited Liability Corporations (LLC). In fact, I have yet to know a project that isn't financed, constructed, or operated by an LLC.

Lifestyle Lost

This form of company operates solely on the operating revenues generated by the corporation. It is a legal entity designed to protect or shelter the external financial assets and resources of the operator or owner. It is a common business structure used for risky investments. When projects created through an LLC cease operation and fail to generate sufficient revenues to cover operational costs, the operating company can go bankrupt, while the owner pulling the strings simply walks away without any financial responsibility. The actual owners and operators behind the LLC can eventually abandon their projects virtually free from any financial obligation to remove the turbines or restore the project site. That responsibility and cost then falls again on the public, which footed most of the bill to build it in the first place.

Ultimately, the taxpayers have paid to create these projects, and they will have to pay again to remove them if and when the lucrative tax subsidies disappear. What better example of government-financed corporate welfare could be devised? Would it surprise you to know that the program that built the current wind energy industry was originally conceived by Enron, a giant energy corporation headquartered in Houston, Texas that collapsed in the early 2000s due to its financial corruption? It happened to be heavily invested in industrial wind energy projects.

Former Mineral County, WV Board of Commissioners President Dr. Wayne Spiggle refers to industrial wind energy as good politics, but bad public policy. When I consider everything I've learned about it, I would have to agree. Is it really so important to rush into industrial wind energy development if it won't generate the benefits it is promoted to confer? What has happened to our capacity for critical thinking and reasoned debate? I am fond of saying that a rush to a solution is a rush to judgment with the added potential for unintended consequences that we may later regret—assuming we can still afford to make those costly mistakes.

****

Throughout my career in planning, I have seen both the best and the worst elements of modern society. The society I moved into when I left the farm to begin college is capable of great technological and humanitarian accomplishments. It has built what can arguably be called the wealthiest and most profitable economy that the world has ever seen, but I have also learned that its successes have come at a great price.

Our society appears to be unable to achieve these benefits without compromising our most basic values. Abuses of privilege and power are increasingly commonplace. Both prominent and influential politicians (at all levels of government) and corporate executives routinely fall prey to greed and avarice. Many feel invulnerable to accountability. Numerous large and successful corporations have collapsed from corruption and fiscal mismanagement. The list of victims reads like the pages of Fortune Magazine.

In the past fifteen years alone, we have seen large corporations representing a wide range of economic sectors fall, including Enron (as I mentioned earlier), WorldCom, HealthSouth, Lehman Brothers, Countrywide, Solyndra, MF Global, and most infamously, Bernie Madoff's investment firm. Over the course of my career, I have seen elected officials and state agency officials take unfair and inappropriate advantage of their positions or authority. You can even look to the acknowledged indiscretions of prominent religious leaders, including the likes of Jimmy Swaggert, Jim Baker, and an ever-expanding litany of priests in the Catholic Church who have violated their own moral principles. It often seems that no segment of society or our economy is immune from the corruption of values that seems to arise from our unbridled lust for greed, power, and wealth.

From my experience and observations, the most common underlying factor seems to be the scale of operation. I consider my own sentiments to be a rejection of "big"—big government agencies, big businesses, big programs, and big institutions. It seems as though anything that grows into something truly big learns to minimize its concerns about individual needs, becomes unable to adapt and resistant to change, and develops a sense of superiority and/or invulnerability that appears to be a natural outgrowth of increased power and authority. Republicans and Democrats tend to divide the political spectrum along public versus private interests. Republicans espouse the wonders of the free market, and in doing so, embrace the interests of big business. Democrats extol the virtues of government to protect the interests of common people, many of whom don't always succeed in life, despite the assistance they may receive. In doing so, they end up embracing the interests of big government.

I find myself dividing the political agenda along different philosophical lines based on the scale of operation. My experience has taught me that *small* government, *small* businesses, and *small* institutions serve the needs of individuals best, even as they may not achieve the best economy of scale. Our economy has simply become so dependent on growth (both in terms of population and wealth) to sustain itself that it essentially forces society's basic institutions to become big, regardless of the consequences that may have on individuality and personal choice.

Our laws are supposed to protect people from monopolies, but what does it really mean when companies can grow to the point that the president proclaims they are "too large to fail?" Is it possible that large businesses have found new ways to grow into effective monopolies and evade the specter or consequences of failure in the competitive market? When you look at the level of control that some big businesses, like Wal-Mart and Microsoft, can exert on market prices and its suppliers, it really forces me to wonder. How does this level of consumer market control and influence fit within the concept of the free market?

We still extol our society's ethical and moral virtues, regardless of how little substance they appear to have in light of what is occurring around us. I have highlighted in detail a number of examples that I have seen throughout my life, and I'm still only scratching the surface. I could talk about many other examples, but I feel I've said enough to make my point. I don't believe I have enough time and energy to discuss it all.

I have come to see the modern society I moved into more than 30 years ago as a society of dependency. It is dependent on big institutions and companies to manage its massive scale. Its people are dependent on money and the accumulation of wealth as a measure of success and to survive. We have become so specialized in our work and daily routines that we are dependent on others to provide the most basic services we can't or don't have the time to provide for ourselves. Many people have simply become dependent on society to take care of them. All of these dependencies undermine the values of self-reliance and independence that I learned as a child. This is the crisis of conscience I have battled for 30 years in trying to decide who I am and how I should live. Now that I have found a way to understand it all and accept my own basic personal values, I have come to the point where I want more independence in my life.

I'm not sure I can say what the future of the society of dependency will be. It is clearly *capable* of generating greater wealth and personal convenience than the society of self-reliance that I experienced as a child. Planners struggle today to make our modern society and communities more sustainable, but they don't seem to consider whether they are truly or ultimately sustainable from an economic perspective. We are currently mired in a deep economic recession that has displaced millions of workers, impoverished a growing number of families, destroyed many of its largest businesses and corporations, and devastated the housing market. Historic evidence from prior great economic collapses suggests that recovery occurs when some major event triggers an explosion of economic growth and prosperity. The Great Depression of the 1930s lingered into the early 1940s, until World War II triggered an expansion of the economy and turned society around.

After thinking extensively about our current economic situation, I really can't identify a specific influence or major source of growth that could quickly turn our economy around. What will trigger the next wave of economic expansion? Our population is already straining the ability of our natural resources to support it. Our government has extended so many taxpayer dollars to the ailing private sector that it has little remaining resources to further stimulate the economy. We are already engaged in an expensive decade-long war on terrorism that is wearing on public acceptance and has done little to improve our safety and security. We have already tapped most of the inexpensive and easily accessible natural resources available to us to fuel our economy. What else remains to trigger the next surge of economic growth that will pull us out of this recession? I certainly don't have an answer to that question. Perhaps that is why so many government officials and leading economists say that the recovery, whatever form it takes, will be long and protracted. And, to think that ultimately, we may only have our unbridled greed and unquenchable thirst for power or control to blame for it all. I certainly don't have any confidence that the planning community can find a sustainable solution for that.

As I now see it, there is no certainty that the modern economy (and its society of dependency) will persevere and survive. Impressive and dominant societies have completely failed in the past. During its time, the Roman Empire was far more superior in every way to the other societies around it than ours is today. It dominated the global economy for at least 400 years before it eventually disappeared. There is building evidence to suggest that the Minoan society that preceded Rome by at least 1,000 years was every bit as economically dominant, and we are only beginning to understand that today. The ancient Egyptian society dominated the world before that.

Our economy has only really dominated the world economy since World War II. If it's this sick after only 60 years of true economic and geo-political dominance, what hard evidence or proof exists, other than our own ego-centric confidence and national pride, that it will be inevitably sustainable over the next 100 years? If I had the kind of crystal ball that could answer that question, my book would read much differently, and I certainly wouldn't be struggling to survive in it.

I believe that I can understand the frustrations and anger expressed by the anti-austerity protests in Europe, the Occupy Wall Street protests in New York and other major cities, and the Tea Party loyalists across the country. I can't say I entirely agree with either their rationales or their professed solutions, but I do feel I understand what has *caused* their frustrations. I would assert that a fundamental disenchantment with big institutions, from big government to big business plays a central role in their protests. I would suggest that they all should consider living a more self-reliant lifestyle, and we'll see just how much philosophical integrity they have.

I simply don't believe that these groups can resolve their frustrations as long as the solutions they advocate are defined by pro-business or pro-government responses. To me, they are all merely reflections of the ongoing political tug-of-war between hard, fast, and inflexible Republican and Democratic party platforms and ideologies that have been used to define social issues for generations. Why else would our politics be mired in divisive ideological gridlock? Neither side wants to change or lose. If it's time to think differently about how we live, then why isn't it time to think differently about how we *define* the political landscape? At what point in the evolution of our society will we decide to focus seriously on our core values and to rebuild our lifestyle and guiding institutions from that foundation? These are the questions that I can't answer on my own, but must ask of you.

As I said at the beginning of my book, you are free to form your own opinions on anything I have said. I don't profess to have all the answers; I am only speaking on the basis of what I have seen and learned over the course of my own life. We all have different life experiences to draw upon in deciding what our society is and how we should live within it. I can certainly respect that. I can also say that I am comfortable with my own assessment of what I have told you, and I can assert that it is based on a strong foundation of critical thinking guided by a healthy measure of logic. I hope you will choose to apply your own critical thinking when evaluating my thoughts and views. I have asked many questions in my writings to trigger that thought process.

V. Coming Full Circle

Driving west on Interstate 66 in northern Virginia from the Capital Beltway (I-495), you will first encounter twenty or so miles of intense, placeless suburban sprawl until it eventually begins to taper off around the Haymarket exit (Exit 40). As you continue west, just beyond mile marker 38, you will cross over a railroad right-of-way, followed on the right by an old plantation farmhouse that was converted into a nursery, and the old stone Chapman's Mill (which was being gradually restored in 2007). Just beyond the mill, you will pass through the first foothill gap of the Blue Ridge Mountains and into what appears to be the rural hinterland beyond metropolitan Washington, DC. Suddenly, the landscape changes dramatically over this 2.5-mile stretch of freeway, and you are welcomed into a forested, rugged mountain countryside colorfully accented by brilliant yellow daffodils along both sides of the freeway in March and April and a pastel sea of white and pink cosmos in the median throughout the summer months.

This was the route that Barb and I often followed to escape our hectic and stressful life in Charles County and retreat into the peaceful and serene rural Appalachian Mountain setting we have enjoyed throughout our life together. We started taking trips to Shenandoah National Park to drive the Skyline Drive within the first couple of months after moving to Charles County. Gradually, over time, we began to explore farther west beyond the Shenandoah Valley itself and into the rugged Allegheny Mountains of West Virginia. I have always needed to spend time in the Appalachian Mountains no matter where I have lived.

During our initial explorations of the Blue Ridge Mountains, I always took note of the landmarks I described above as familiar milestones marking the transition into a truly rural environment. At least, that's certainly how it appeared during the daylight. However, our first trip along that stretch of highway between Haymarket and Front Royal *after* sunset gave me a very different impression. In the daylight, all you can see from the highway is forested hillsides, broken sporadically by a few old farm fields and widely scattered homes and meadows. At night, the dark and forested hills are illuminated like Christmas trees by the glow of hundreds upon hundreds of street and yard lights.

As it turns out, this section of Interstate 66 is not a truly rural area at all. It is a battleground in the ongoing struggle between the former, traditional, rural economy of the Blue Ridge Mountains and the expanding ex-urban Washington, DC economy as the mountain woodlands are devoured by residential tract subdivisions. You just can't see all the houses during the daylight, because they are all tucked securely into the remaining woods. There they sit, patiently waiting for an opportunity to pounce into another unsuspecting section of woodlands or a former farm, which will be quickly devoured into another development of two-to-three acre house lots for urban-dwellers seeking their own little piece of what they vainly consider to be their slice of wilderness.

This competition for space and dominance is just another chapter in the continuing battle between the former society of self-reliance and the extravagant, technology-driven society of dependency. The standard battle cry is, "resistance is futile," (as the Borg from television's *Star Trek: The Next Generation* would boldly proclaim), and it echoes constantly and brazenly throughout the hills and hollows. Its message is alluring to some and frightening to others. Eventually, the remaining self-reliant people will either be assimilated into the new social order or will retreat deeper into the mountains. We consciously decided to take the latter course of action.

When I explained our plans for our retirement property, my friend Frank O'Hara coined a term for it that a friend described to him as "voluntary simplicity." As his friend explained it, this means that we plan to employ simple traditional technologies and folkways as a voluntary lifestyle choice. I like the concept he uses, but I think I would characterize our lifestyle choice more precisely as "*strategic* simplicity." I *do* plan to utilize modern technologies, some of which were not as efficient and some of which were not even available when I was growing up.

For example, solar energy technology is far more sophisticated and advantageous than the simpler passive and low-power photovoltaic systems that I saw being employed by self-reliant, back-to-the-land purists when I was growing up in the Upper Valley. Likewise, pellet stoves had not been invented, yet they are a far cleaner, efficient, and persistent source of heat than the traditional woodstove. In my concept of a self-reliant lifestyle (as I explained earlier), modern or advanced technology does not necessarily diminish independent living *if* it makes it easier, more efficient, or less expensive to achieve self-reliance.

To emphasize this point, I'm sure the horse-drawn corn planter we once used was a significant advancement in technology from the hand planting techniques that the earliest pioneers used. However, its introduction didn't create a dependency on money or additional technologies. It did, however, make it easier, more efficient, and more cost-effective for later farmers to plant corn. It also improved their yields. As a result, this simple technological advancement actually enhanced their ability to live independently and to prosper from it.

Too many of the technological advancements in our society, like video games and DVD players, do nothing to empower self-reliant living; they only make users more dependent on money to buy games or movies and on other specialists to design and manufacture them. In that respect, they create a greater addiction to the modern economy. Video games have no useful benefit to people who seek to minimize their dependency on the outside economy and live a simpler, more independent lifestyle.

In using the term *strategic simplicity* to define my desired lifestyle choice, I intend to strategically select and use only those modern technological improvements that make it easier and more feasible for us to achieve as much economic independence in our retirement as possible. We are working to reduce our basic cost of living by eliminating debt and using the barter system to expand our limited purchasing power. We will work to produce our own food using our land resources wisely. We want to eliminate unnecessary conveniences that only increase our cost of living and promote a listless and unhealthy lifestyle. We can't control health care costs, but we can live a healthier and more productive physically active lifestyle. We can also learn to use old traditional remedies to help reduce our need for expensive drugs.

These strategies, in sum total, represent the strategic simplicity practices that we are working to employ to return to a more self-reliant and truly sustainable life. In essence, the vain excesses of the materialistic and consumptive modern society have convinced me that it is inherently better, healthier, and more rewarding to return to a self-reliant lifestyle than to casually accept life in the society of dependency. I simply refuse to be assimilated into a lifestyle driven by an endless pursuit of greater wealth to get or stay ahead of the rapidly escalating cost of a modern standard of living.

I believe that the middle class in this country has been trapped in that relentless chase for far too long, and all that its people have to show for it is greater debt and a rented lifestyle, from the homes they live in to the furniture they acquire to fill it. This is the economic situation that fuels so much of the frustration that we see arising out of the Great Recession. Materialism, the accumulation of wealth at any cost, and the unbridled greed that fuels it all appear to be undermining the very fabric of the economy as well as the ethical fabric of our society. Even Alan Greenspan, the former chairman of the Federal Reserve Board, eventually admitted (but only after *leaving* the Federal Reserve Board) that he had failed to take into account the influence of greed in deciding how best to manage and stimulate the economy. In the end, he was finally right. Unfortunately for the uncounted millions who are suffering from the Great Recession, his epiphany came too late. I highly doubt that his standard of living has suffered as greatly.

For more than 60 years, the society of dependency has trounced the traditional society of self-reliance into submission or outright defeat on every battleground it has chosen. It is happening in the Shenandoah Valley as I write these words. However, I feel that I'm now seeing a fundamental weakness in the strength, resiliency, and sustainability of the modern economy and the society it supports. Perhaps, as Alan Greenspan was forced to realize, greed will ultimately become the seed of its own demise. All I can tell you for sure is that industrial wind energy will never save it.

I just wonder about all the people who have become so dependent on our modern economy for their sustenance and survival. How will they survive if the mighty American or global economy does collapse? What if there is no economic fuel left in the world to revive it? How will people feel if or when Americans begin to starve at the levels that draw international attention and sympathy for people in Africa? It is my inability to answer these fundamental questions that has driven me back full circle to the lifestyle that raised me. We lived on the edge of poverty and never realized it. We survived and managed to achieve some measure of success in the outside world. It is that basic ingenuity, ambition, determination, and perseverance that I draw upon today to make the transition back to a more self-reliant lifestyle. I can't say it will protect me from a complete collapse of the modern global economy, but it may make it easier and more feasible to survive. If you are interested in understanding how I hope to achieve it, I'll explain it to you.

****

In early April 2006, Barb and I took our first trip into the Potomac Highlands region of West Virginia. We crossed into the state over North Mountain on WV Route 55 near Wardensville. From there, we traveled to Moorefield, then picked up U.S. Route 220 and headed south through Petersburg to Franklin. After a brief tour of Franklin village, we turned east onto U.S. Route 33 and exited the state crossing over Shenandoah Mountain on the way to Harrisonburg, VA. We stopped briefly in Moorefield, Franklin, and Harrisonburg to pick up real estate guides. We were scouting out areas where we might like to find some retirement property, just as we had done in the North Georgia mountains more than a dozen years earlier.

I must admit, we were not especially impressed with our first tour through the region. We arrived in the state at the tail end of winter, just a week or two before everything started turning green. The landscape appeared dull, worn, and lifeless from a long, snowy winter. It had turned warm that day, but the skies bore a gray overcast that magnified the browns in the sleeping landscape. Still, we were quite impressed with the villages of Moorefield, Petersburg, and Franklin, and we thought they might hold some promise for us. Barb was especially impressed with the Route 33 scenic overlook at the summit of Shenandoah Mountain on the West Virginia/Virginia state line. The distant views of ridgeline upon ridgeline reminded her of Vermont, where we had met and married in 1991.

The land prices listed in the real estate guides we collected on that trip encouraged me to look more intensely in the neighboring states. We picked up real estate guides in north central Pennsylvania during a summer trip to Niagara Falls, Ontario. We also traveled to Cumberland, MD on Labor Day weekend to look for property in western Maryland. In the interim, I searched the Internet and made telephone inquiries to realtors in the Asheville, North Carolina area, which we fell in love with while visiting from Alabama. All those efforts only proved that we would find our best values in eastern West Virginia.

Our West Virginia search intensified. We made two additional trips in the third week of September and on Columbus Day weekend in 2006. We drove extensively through Randolph, Pocahontas, Tucker, Grant, Hardy, and Pendleton Counties touring properties that we found in real estate magazines and on the Internet. We subscribed briefly to the Elkins, WV newspaper, the *InterMountain,* to peruse the real estate listings. After visiting about a dozen different properties, we found the one we wanted and eventually purchased our property in the Pendleton County community of Brushy Run. On November 17, 2006, we signed the deed and took ownership. We have never looked back since.

The property is not large, comprising a little over six acres of a former farm field that had been subdivided in 2000. Lots within the subdivision range in size from small, two-acre recreational (non-year-round) lots deeper into the forest that carpets the flanks of Cave Mountain to much larger lots over ten acres in size. While our lot was small, the fact that the majority of the land was an active hayfield made it easy to locate and prepare a nice house site. Even after dedicating some of the field to a house, we would still retain enough cultivated land for a large garden and a small agricultural enterprise, if we could identify a use that would bring good value for the limited acreage. After deciding on the house site, we determined that between 3.5 and 4.5 acres of open land remained.

A small portion of this land will be dedicated to a large garden where we can grow a large variety of our own herbs, vegetables, and ground fruits. We plan to make the garden large enough to provide more food than we will need in the summer months, with the expectation that we will can the leftovers to carry us through the winter. We can supplement our own garden production with the natural fruits of the land. Our subdivision is adjoined on two sides by the Monongahela National Forest, and two walking trails lead directly into the National Forest property and up the eastern slopes of Cave Mountain. Within the forest, we can find a wide variety of natural herbs, plants, nuts, and berries that we can freely harvest. A number of these plants have value for traditional medicines. We simply need to learn more about these wild plants and roots and how to make use of them.

While protein remains a challenge, I can learn to hunt. Many of our neighbors take advantage of the plentiful deer herd that exists in the National Forest. We have found venison to be a good source of meat that can be used to supplement our diet in a number of ways. Fishing is another option. The South Branch of the Potomac River runs through Smoke Hole Canyon on the opposite side of Cave Mountain from our property and is a very popular fishing location. Through the strategic use of the natural resources that abound around us, we have a number of options we can pursue to supplement the productive limitations of our property and our financial resources to support our dietary needs. If you wish to live self-reliantly on a small property, it helps to have protected public lands nearby that can be used to serve your remaining needs. West Virginia offers these opportunities in great abundance.

As for the remaining balance of our land, I am pursuing ways to make it economically productive. Doing so will provide additional income for us as well as physical labor to help keep us active and healthy. My first thought is to establish a home-based wine-making operation. Although I have no experience in this type of operation, I know it could be done profitably on small plots of land, and it seemed like a reasonable activity for the land we owned. Our property is located on an open and sunny southeast-facing slope in one of the driest areas of West Virginia during the summertime. Upper Tract, a community roughly five miles south of our property, receives the lowest average annual rainfall of any community in the state. This setting and rainfall pattern represents some of the most favorable wine-making conditions that West Virginia has to offer.

Also, in discovering my biological family, I learned that my great-grandfather owned and operated a small winery in Transylvania before immigrating to western Pennsylvania at the end of the nineteenth century. Wine-making had been a traditional pursuit in my biological family and is an important aspect of my family's cultural heritage. An operation of this nature would not only be a reasonable and suitable economic pursuit for the land we purchased. It would also pay homage to both my agricultural upbringing and, more specifically, my biological family's heritage.

We also began planting some apple trees, and we intend to plant a few peach trees as well. We wanted to raise some other essential fruits besides grapes that we could use to make homemade jellies and desserts. If we do eventually establish a wine-making operation on the property, I also intend to raise some honey bees. The bees would be beneficial in pollinating our fruit trees and grapes, and they would also produce honey, which we could use as a natural sweetener and as a basic ingredient in making a traditional mead wine. All of these ancillary agricultural activities can be feasibly conducted on our modest retirement property.

We haven't concluded that our future agricultural pursuit will be a wine-making operation. We are considering other agricultural avenues suitable for smaller properties, such as raising dairy goats, sheep, and/or alpacas. We also realize that we could establish a home-based woodworking craft operation. I have acquired virtually all of the tools I would need by building our own house. Barb has considered quilting as a way to turn a cherished hobby into a source of supplemental income. Barb's banking and finance skills are also potential marketable services. Whatever we finally decide to do with our land or skills must allow us to earn some additional cash to satisfy our most basic needs that we simply can't provide for ourselves, due to our specific land limitations.

Fortunately, we don't have to convert all of our products or services into currency. We may be able to barter or trade some of them for eggs, milk, or other essentials that we don't have the acreage to produce for ourselves. Our primary objective is to live a healthy and active retirement lifestyle that will permit us to live as self-reliantly as possible. I'm not a person who wants to pay for a gym membership to keep myself in shape; I'd rather do productive physical labor to produce our own food, maintain our property, and earn what little additional cash we might need to survive.

As long as we minimize the number of outside services we need (and the resulting monthly bills they generate), we can manage our essential cost of living at a level that would be sustainable on a very low income. You don't need to earn much money to survive, if you don't generate a lot of expenses. This is the lesson I learned growing up on the farm, and it remains the main reason why one can live comfortably and satisfactorily on a poverty-level income. This is the fundamental model of self-reliant living that I understand, internalize, and endorse. It provides an honest living that removes me from most of the ethical challenges and dilemmas I face in the modern society that have caused much of my discontent with that lifestyle. I simply have no fear of working harder to gain the freedom and peace of mind that I seek to achieve from my professional retirement. If the planning profession truly offered me a successful economic pursuit, I feel it should at least finance my efforts to achieve that ultimate satisfaction.

In 2009, we began building our own retirement house on the property to ensure that we will not have any mortgage or loan to pay off when we finally retire. In fact, if we manage our expenses over time according to our plans, we will be entirely debt-free when we finally leave and sell our current home in New Creek, WV. We work at our primary jobs during the week, then travel on weekends, holidays, and vacations to our retirement property in Pendleton County to work on the house. Of course, we have had to hire contractors to help with certain elements of the construction work that we simply could not do more affordably on our own or are simply beyond our means, such as installing the septic system and well, excavating and pouring the foundation walls, erecting the exterior walls, setting the roof trusses, and installing interior wiring. However, my wife and I (with some help from our son) have done all of the additional work that we are technically and physically capable of doing, and we have worked alongside most of our contractors.

I didn't have any prior experience in homebuilding, but my retirement property neighbor, Maynard Tingley, worked for many years as a residential contractor, and he has been generous enough to teach me what I don't know. He and his wife, Irene, have become our best friends in Brushy Run. Maynard is originally from northern Maine, and we share many stories of our experiences growing up in rural New England. He and some of his relatives helped us erect the exterior framing and roofing during the first year. In exchange for his help and guidance, we have returned the favor by repainting their garage, installing handrails in their bathroom, supplying lumber for and helping build a wheelchair ramp to their back porch, replacing his master bathroom sink, and assisting them with other routine chores. This is the Appalachian tradition of neighborliness and community spirit.

Most of our own construction work has been done using rechargeable power tools (drill, framing and finish nail guns, circular saw, reciprocating saw, etc.). We have supplemented them with simple hand tools. Even after two full years of work, no permanent or temporary electric service has been installed on our property. As I mentioned earlier, we are hoping to eventually power the home using solar panels so that we do not have to be served by the power grid. I haven't yet determined if we can afford to do so, but we are keeping as many power service options open as we can.

Our first priority is to use solar power exclusively, supplemented with batteries to store excess power and an LP gas generator to provide supplemental power to recharge the batteries during extended periods of low solar output. This option allows us the greatest freedom from monthly power bills that we cannot control, but it is very expensive to implement. One of our early acquaintances in Pendleton County, Larry and Kaye Thomas had been using solar energy to help power their home for several years. They were unable to rely exclusively on solar energy because the high ridges on the east and west sides of their home reduced their direct sun exposure to only four hours per day. Fortunately, the solar exposure of our retirement home is much better. If we can successfully power our home this way, we will end up with what I fondly call our nineteenth century home in the twenty-first century. Our house would essentially sit alone on the land with no connection to an external infrastructure system—no public water, no public sewer, no telephone line, and no electric line.

Achieving this level of energy independence will require *extensive* lifestyle sacrifices, and we are working to build into our home redundant systems to manage our demand for electricity. We will have both a wood cookstove and a pellet stove for winter heating. The wood cookstove can help us reduce the need to use an electric stove and/or microwave oven during the winter months, when our power generation potential is much lower.

We are also buying more traditional hand-operated devices, such as a wall mounted, crank can opener, a hand-cranked egg beater, battery-operated clocks, etc. What electrical devices we absolutely need will be as energy-efficient as possible. I don't know if most people understand this, but we waste a lot of electricity with the high technology household devices that we so readily accept as necessities. Do you realize that when you shut off your television, stereo, video game console, or DVD player by remote control it is still consuming electricity? *Anything* you shut down by remote control has to remain partially active (in standby mode) in order to power up when it receives a signal from the remote control. Many other devices also have internal clocks that continue operating after the unit is shut off. How many redundant digital clocks does the average household really need, anyway?

We have learned to connect many of these devices to power strips that can be shut off when the unit is powered down. These power strips provide basic power surge protection and help reduce our need for electricity. To me, if you're concerned about the impacts of our surging electrical demand on the environment, your first course of action should be to reduce or eliminate wasteful and unnecessary consumption. Doing so goes way beyond installing a new heating system or installing extra insulation. It requires a complete reconsideration of how we conduct our daily lives. In fact, we pay additional prices for the technological conveniences we so casually consume in the form of a less healthy lifestyle and higher electric bills. For us, these changes in behavior have become some of the simplest ways we can make our lifestyle more sustainable and self-reliant.

If we eventually determine that we cannot afford to operate our home on solar energy alone, our next choice would be to use net-metering. This form of power service allows us to combine standard power service from the grid with electricity from solar panels. The panels are connected into the electrical system serving the house in such a way that any excess power generated by the panels (over and above the electricity we need and use to power the house) are contributed to the grid, for which we receive a credit on our monthly power service bill for the electricity we generate. Consequently, our monthly electric bills would be significantly lowered. The downside of this system is that we would still receive another monthly bill and, by virtue of the way the solar power contributions to the grid are calculated by the electric company, we may not receive full value for all the excess power we generate.

In April 2011, we toured a home in Fulk's Run, Virginia using a net metered solar energy system. The system requires fewer solar panels and batteries to operate than a stand-alone system would, but it requires additional hardware to separately track both solar energy production and electrical power use from the grid. The overall equipment costs are correspondingly lower and the system allowed them to significantly reduce their monthly power bills. They also have the benefit of reliable and consistent power service through their connection to the grid. The tax credits that they received by purchasing the system helped make it a viable option for them.

Our last resort is standard electric service. I truly hope that it won't come to that, but I also can't control all of the factors, including cost, our limited financial resources, and local technology constraints, that might influence our decision. This is the primary reason why we have postponed installing any electric service as long as we have. Time is the only variable that we can control to keep our options flexible. With any luck, further advancements in solar technology, reduced material costs, and/or potential tax credits will become more beneficial to us the longer we can wait in making our final decision.

****

The plan I have just outlined for you is our basic strategy to return to a more self-reliant lifestyle. There are a lot of little details that we are still working to resolve. Obviously, I can't promise it will work or that we can achieve it precisely according to our plans. That kind of assurance doesn't even exist with our current modern lifestyle. It obviously requires hard work and determination. Hopefully, those are elements I can control. What I can say about it is that it offers us the greatest level of control over the course and conduct of our life. It seems to me that many people who currently struggle in the modern economy to keep pace with a cost of living that is increasingly out of their control would benefit greatly from a similar path. Perhaps it is not as alluring a lifestyle as the more glamorous and extravagant lifestyle of the rich and famous, but that is not a crowd we aspire to join, and it is not a realistic or practical option for us.

However, if that is what you truly want from life, perhaps you should spend more of your limited funds on the lottery. All I can say is that the odds of winning are not in your favor.

Our modern economy operates on the premise that the pursuit of money and wealth in the free market is a variable-sum game. A variable-sum game is one in which the resources you compete for are not finite or limited. They will grow as the economy grows so that those competing for monetary resources don't necessarily limit their competitors' opportunity to earn their share. In other words, I don't have to deprive others from the opportunity to become wealthy or worse yet, to take money from others just for me to become wealthy.

However, the recent economic climate seems to suggest that our market economy, even at the global level, is more of a zero-sum game than theory would suggest. In a zero-sum game, the total resources available to everyone are limited to a specific amount, so that you can only win more for yourself by taking resources away from your competitors. If the economy was truly a variable sum game, why would we need to employ the creative credit practices that contributed to its collapse in order to satisfy our basic needs? It seems as though whenever greed and the desire for wealth greatly exceeds the economy's ability to produce greater wealth, the nature of the game changes from a variable-sum game to a zero-sum game. Perhaps those are conditions that characterize economic booms and recessions.

What I sense today is a global economy that appears to be stuck in the mode of a zero-sum game. It marks a point in time when wealth begins to shift and become concentrated in the hands of those with the greatest level of control or power. This assessment is supported by a September 2011 report entitled, <u>Income, Poverty, and Health Insurance Coverage in the United States: 2010</u>, issued by the U.S. Department of Commerce.[xv] A statement on page 10 of the report reads, "Comparing changes in household income at selected percentiles shows that income inequity is increasing (Table A-3). Between 1999 (the year that household income peaked before the 2001 recession) and 2010, income at the 50th and 10th percentiles declined, 7.1 percent and 12.1 percent respectively, while the decline in income at the 90th percentile was 1.5 percent." I don't feel that I am or can be one of the people who will benefit most from that gradual shift of wealth.

Consequently, I have chosen to pursue a path that gives me a greater chance for economic independence with limited wealth. In these trying times, what more can a person do?

I do hope that some of you who read this story will be encouraged to consider pursuing your own self-reliant lifestyle. After all, it is the only meaningful way that the more traditional folkways (and the society of self-reliance that they support) will survive. Otherwise, the society of self-reliance will simply become another lifestyle lost to history. The unfortunate reality we face from that is the lingering uncertainty that our modern society of dependency is fundamentally more sustainable. What kind of world would we be left with if both options become extinct? It's not just a matter of what you are going to do now, but what you will do then? Hopefully, if I am ultimately successful in my own retirement plans, I will become one of the remaining few who won't have to worry about it. After I am gone and reduced to a fading memory eroded by the restless flow of time, the fate of the society of self-reliance will fall in *your* hands. I feel that's more than enough good food for thought.

ENDNOTES:

[i] <u>Perceptions of Rural America,</u> W.K. Kellogg Foundation, 2002, Ford 4031, Item #830, 1101-1.5M-SCG, page 1.

[ii] Scott E. Hastings, Jr., <u>The Last Yankees</u>, Hanover and London, University Press of New England, 1990, pages xii-xiii.

[iii] Barbara Pash, "Maryland Taking Action as Students Pile Up Loan Debt," *Cumberland Times-News*, October 2, 2011, Vol. 72, No. 271, page 1A.

[iv] Frostburg State University Renewable Energy Center Wind and Solar Energy Demonstration Project, "Small Scale Wind and Solar Energy in Western Maryland," Soysal, O.A and Soysal, H.S., 2008. The data and report are available on the program's web site at http://www.fsuwise.org/renewable/.

[v] The actual formula to calculate how much electricity a wind turbine can produce is: $P = k\ C_p 1/2 dAV^3$, where:

P = power output in kilowatts

k= 0.000133, a mathematical constant to convert the formula's output into kilowatts

C_p= the maximum power coefficient, ranging from 0.25 to 0.45, dimension less d= air density in lb/ft^3

A= the area swept by the turbine's rotor blades in ft^2 or $\pi D^2/4$

V= the wind speed in MPH

as outlined in the handbook <u>Small Wind Electric Systems</u>, produced for the U.S. Department of Energy by the National Renewable Energy Laboratory, January 2007.

[vi] Eileen O'Grady "Loss of Wind Causes Texas Power Grid Emergency," Reuters News Service, February 27, 2008.

[vii] David Lester, "Changes in The Wind: The Ebbs and Flows of Wind Power Stress the Northwest Power Grid," Yakima, WA Herald-Republic, July 25, 2009.

[viii] James Oswald and Michael Raine, <u>UK Renewable Energy Data</u>, Renewable Energy Foundation, December 8, 2006— this report provides monthly electric power generation curves over multiple years for over 100 industrial wind energy projects in Europe.

[ix] Robert Bryce, <u>Gusher of Lies: The Dangerous Delusions of "Energy Independence,"</u> Public Affairs, 2008.

[x] <u>Federal Financial Interventions and Subsidies in Energy Markets 2007</u>, SR/CNEAF/2008-01, Energy Information Administration, Office of Coal, Nuclear, Electric, and Alternate Fuels, U.S. Department of Energy, April 2008, page 16.

[xi] White House Briefing Memo, Subject--Renewable Energy Loan Guaranties and Grants, October 25, 2010, From Carol Browner, Ron Klain, and Larry Summers to President Obama, page 8.

[xii] "Wind Making Great Strides as Energy Provider," Kristi E Swartz, Palm Beach, FL Post News, October 7, 2007.

[xiii] Jake Tapper, "General Electric Paid No Corporate Taxes in 2010," ABC World News, March 25, 2011. See the ABC News website at http://abcnews.go.com/Politics/general-electric-paid-federal-taxes-2010/story?id=13224558 for additional details.

[xiv] Robert Bryce, "America's Worst Wind-Energy Project," October 12, 2011, National Review Online.

[xv] Income, Poverty, and Health Insurance Coverage in the United States: 2010, Current Population Reports, P60-239, September, 2011, U.S. Government Printing Office, Washington, DC.